A LIGHTER SHADE OF BLUE

A LIGHTER SHADE OF BLUE

The Lighthearted Memoirs of
an Air Marshal

Christopher Foxley-Norris

LONDON
IAN ALLAN LTD

First published 1978

ISBN 0 7110 0858 2

Published by Ian Allan Ltd, Shepperton, Surrey, and printed in the United Kingdom by Crampton & Sons Ltd, Sawston, Cambridge

Contents

1   Pinfeathers

In writing my story I was faced with a choice between two alternatives; whether to be strictly factual and historical; or whether to attempt to be reasonably entertaining. Readers may determine for themselves which choice I made.

I am convinced, and will remain so to my dying day, that my first, and presumably formative encounter with powered flight, occurred in Hull towards the end of World War I. I have a vivid memory of my nurse holding me up to the window to ' watch the pretty Zeppelin lit up by the searchlights '. The fact that every member of the family denies that any such incident ever occurred; the fact that any nanny so imperilling her charge would have been instantly dismissed; and indeed the fact that we certainly could not afford a nanny at the time, do nothing to shake my profound belief in this recollection. The Zeppelin had large black crosses at each end, as I recall, and buzzed like a wasp in a jam-jar.

Whatever the rights and wrongs of this matter, my interest in aviation then lapsed for a number of years. I chanted ' Amy, wonderful Amy ' with the best of them as Miss Johnson busily traversed the oceans; and I myself was bold enough to circumnavigate a local meadow in the back seat of some Heath Robinson contrivance of Alan Cobham's Flying Circus. But otherwise the seed lay dormant, until my arrival at Oxford in 1935.

This is not to say, however, that my life at the time was totally devoid of military interest. Like all other public school boys of my age, I was conscripted into ' the Corps ', which at that time of course was strictly Armyoriented and never dreamed of today's RAF or Naval sections of Combined Cadet Forces. I was only an adequate private soldier, being prone to puttee-collapse at critical moments, but I managed to pass the obligatory Certificate A (' Your section is pinned down by heavy mortar and howitzer fire and the enemy is using both chlorine and mustard gas. A large body of enemy scouts has infiltrated to your rear and brigades of heavy cavalry are threatening both your flanks. What action do you take? '). At this period I ill-timedly fell under the spell of Mr Beverly Nichol's anti-war book *Cry Havoc;* and reported myself to the Second Master as a convinced pacifist and conscientious objector. The omens for a career in the Armed Forces did not seem promising.

On such occasions, a transfer to the Boy Scouts was customary, but here too my performance lacked something in the event. I was quite successful as a fire-lighter and knot-tier, and was in fact put in charge of a patrol; this proved my undoing. Until then (aetat 16/17) my experience of alcohol was confined to a ritual small bottle of Whiteway's Cider, consumed with some ceremony at luncheon on each birthday. Thus, when I was one evening leading my patrol back to our summer camp in Wales, exhausted and dehydrated, it was a natural instinct to turn into what proved to be a primitive village hostelry and sustain them with a flagon or two of the same. In the event, sharing my inexperience in the matter, they each cheerfully consumed two pints of rough; and later that evening I faced my first (and I hope last) accusation of drunk in charge—not of a car of course but of what proved to be an equally drunken patrol. A unique occasion, but again perhaps not wholly auspicious.

I duly completed my education at what, even by contemporary standards, was a particularly monastic public school, where the idea of sex played no part in our scheme of things. My own ignorance was accentuated by the fact that I had been left fatherless at the age of five. Thus it was with a background of unique naiveté and inexperience that in the autumn of 1935 I attended my first sherry party in a friend's house at Oxford whither I had graduated. Peering ' across a crowded room ' I detected something that at once attracted my attention and took my fancy; and I enquired of a bystander what it might be.

' That ', he said, ' is a female—a girl in fact '.

' Oh! ', I replied, ' that's nice. I feel I should like to have one. How does one set about it? '

' Well ', he told me, ' the first thing you need is a car, what with the Dean and the Proctors and all that '.

I was properly dished and downcast. To buy a car, even in those days, one required some small capital and, as a scholarship boy, I had none. The prospects appeared gloomy so, as was my practice in such circumstances, I sought advice from my brother. He was two years ahead of me in age, experience and University residence; and among his contemporaries enjoyed an enviable and well merited reputation as a sophisticate and all round roué. As ever, he did not fail me.

' What you should do ', he suggested, ' is apply to join the Oxford University Air Squadron. If you are accepted you will be commissioned in the Reserve of Air Force Officers, which carries with it an engagement grant of £25—quite enough to buy yourself a car and get on with things '.

I was quick to follow this admirable counsel; and here we are today. Omnia vincit amor.

Perhaps I should not close this episode without mentioning that I was thus enabled to purchase for £13 a splendid 5-year old Lea-Francis, which admirably met what I have since learnt to call ' the object of the exercise ' by having a bench front-seat, suitably unimpeded by having both handbrake and gear lever mounted to the right of the steering wheel. Performance (the car's, that is) was admirable and I eventually sold it for £12 in 1939, giving a satisfactory depreciation rate of five shillings per annum; I was naturally sorry to learn that it blew up in total mechanical disintegration before the new owner had completed 50 miles—a touch of Beth Gelert here?

8

My three years with the Oxford University Air Squadron were enjoyable and interesting, and eventually proved valuable. I was only an average pilot and gave my instructors a certain amount of trouble. I presented the first of them, Flight Lieutenant Jimmy Kirkpatrick, with a particular problem. I had learnt from other people on the Squadron that it was customary during the very first air experience flight for the pupil to be invited by the instructor to nominate any particular manoeuvre he would like to experience. Pondering on this, I realized that I had no evidence as to whether I should take to flying at all, and indeed might prove to be frightened of the whole unnatural business. I concluded that the best thing to do might be to ask for something really terrifying the first time, so that everything else would seem mild and acceptable thereafter. Consequently when the customary invitation came over the speaking tube, I asked to be shown an inverted spin (in this a normal spin is carried out with the aircraft 'inside out' and the crew are subjected to a large amount of negative gravity). After a short hesitation and a couple of abortive attempts my instructor duly complied, and my aim was certainly attained in full measure. Nevertheless I enjoyed the rest of the flight sufficiently to commit myself and duly accepted the King's shilling—or rather £25.

Years later, Jimmy confided in me that this was also the first time he himself had ever conducted that particular manoeuvre; and that consequently any terror felt was entirely mutual; but at least we both lived to tell the tale.

Like most other student pilots I had some other alarming experiences. My first and very short solo cross-country was due to terminate at Manston in Kent and I arrived overhead in beautiful weather, which had attracted a number of the resident Air Force officers to take their midday gin on the lawn, which immediately overlooked the grass airfield. In those old-fashioned days of biplanes, the glide approach was de rigueur and I duly (as I thought) closed the throttle and floated in to land. Having involuntarily landed two or three times in effect, I then floated off again and staggered round, somewhat mystified, for another attempt. This proved equally abortive and hair-raising and by the time I was making my fourth essay, I was playing to a packed house on the Officers' Mess Lawn, where heavy odds were by now being laid against the survival of the intrepid visiting aeronaut. During my final approach I solved the mystery. Some minor defect had developed in the throttle quadrant, so that the lever was catching slightly in the half open position; which was in fact as far as I had managed to move it until then. Slamming it fully closed, I finally found mother earth with some relief.

I was met by a stony faced Squadron Leader (presumably he had been laying some of those heavy bets) who enquired the name of my unit and my instructor and reached for the telephone. On my eventual return my reception was equally frosty.

However, by the grace of God one survived; and in the process moved into the magical world of true open cockpit flying, of formation, aerobatics, stalls and side-slips and practice forced landings in and out of wind (' if ever

9

you have to do a real one, my boy, look around for a herd of cows below you—if there's any wind, they'll be pointing their backsides into it '). One made some progress in the art and even acquired some expertise, graduating to the Hawker Hart—still a biplane but also then still a front line squadron aircraft. And one made friends. There is nothing like a shared experience of adventure, excitement and challenge to form and cement young friendships. We flew together, and criticized each other's aerobatics; we drank together, and sympathized with mutual hangovers; we talked and sometimes even gave a moment's thought to what might lie for us over the clouding horizon.

Lifelong friendships. But how sadly in so many cases the life was not long. Alex Obolensky; Mike Marshal; Richard Hillary; Melvin (Dinghy) Young; Noel Agazarian. So many others who went so quickly and so prematurely. Of all my friends, perhaps the most improbable survivor because the most hare-brained risk-taker was Leonard Cheshire, who proved even more improbably in later life to be consecutively the greatest bomber pilot of the War and perhaps the best candidate for canonization of our generation. If someone had told me then that 40 years later I should find myself Chairman of a global charitable foundation, maintaining 180 homes for the sick and the relief of suffering and founded by the selfsame Cheshire, I doubt if I would have given him much credence.

In 1939 one's days, however, could still be carefree and it was with real regret that I finally left the University and its Air Squadron. Having won a Harmsworth Scholarship to the Middle Temple I had stayed up at Oxford an extra year to read for the Bar; and thereafter I moved to London to read for my Finals. I also planned to join No 615 (County of Surrey) Auxiliary Squadron to continue my flying, if they would have me, for the Auxiliary Air Force was a corps d'élite, and competition to join was intense.

But greater men were making larger plans in wider fields, and mine duly went the way of those of mice and men.

2 Overture and Prelude

Although certain optimistic ostriches both in public and private life continued to buy their heads in the sand and turn their blind ends to the reality of the gathering storm, to most of us war had become something inevitable as the months of 1939 passed. When we discussed it, the question was 'when?' not 'whether?'; and our reactions varied with our characters and personalities. Some, the bold, the adventurous, the realistic (and perhaps the hypocritical) looked forward to a resolution of the issue; for some reason everybody assumed that when the conflict came it could not in any sense resemble the long drawn out bloodbath of World War I but must be short and decisive. Perhaps much of this was wishful thinking; the idea of another Somme, another Passchendaele, another Verdun was unthinkable and was therefore rejected. But inevitably we airmen were influenced by the teachings of Douhet and his followers and the propaganda of the school of thought that ' the bomber will always get through ' (so it often did in the event, at least when used at night, but for a long while it usually got through to the wrong place; when it got through it didn't know where it was; and when it did bomb the target the bombs missed). We accepted that airpower could knock out cities, industries and communications; and that populations could not withstand sustained bombing. The side that could hit hardest and maintain its hitting power would soon force the surrender of the other; or so we confidently believed.

We were young and we were wrong; but a lot of other people who were older and should have been wiser were just as wrong, and with less excuse. They deceived us with their propaganda, but they also deceived themselves by believing it.

In this atmosphere it was with no surprise that at the end of August I received instructions from the Air Ministry to report to the RAF station at Hullavington for advanced flying training. On comparing notes with my friends in the same class of Reserve, I found I had been lucky. The great majority, including my brother, had been told to proceed to various ground-training units mostly by the seaside, where they spent the winter marching briskly up and down the promenades to the admiration of the local ladies and, presumably, the consternation and deterrence of any potential invader.

This strange organization became known as Critchley's Private Army, after the well publicized retired Brigadier who was given charge of it (perhaps to keep him out of greater mischief). Under his aegis, to them were soon added a weird mixture of great names from the sporting scene, pugilists like Len Harvey, golfers like Henry Cotton and other eminences from the world of football and racing. On one memorable occasion, a powerful figure launched a formal protest to the officer in charge of a parade.

' 'Ere, wot's this? This ain't good enough. These stripes just make me a Sergeant. I ought to be an orficer.'

' And what ' (plum in mouth and amused smile), ' my good man, makes you think you have the qualities required for a commission? '

' It's nothin' to do with what I think, mate, Critch *said* I could be an orficer '.

And it was so.

We luckier people counted our blessings; but I had a personal problem. I had been in the middle of an intensive cramming course when I was called to the colours and my Bar Finals were a mere six weeks away. It seemed a pity that all my hard work and all my mother's considerable sacrifices to get me to that penultimate stage should be wasted. With an impudence which makes me shudder when I think of it today, I accordingly asked for an interview with my Station Commander. This was granted and Group Captain Elliott-Smith (bear in mind that in those days Group Captains were great and terrifying figures in the Air Force world: you went and hid behind a hut if you saw one approaching) not only listened kindly to my plea for a six weeks' postponement but even forwarded it to the Air Ministry authorities. There, however, even greater men firmly rejected it on the well accepted grounds that all out aerial warfare (the word ' blitz ' was not yet in general use) was about to burst on us and every qualified pilot would be needed in the line.

So I returned to my operational training, concentrating earnestly on navigation, procedural attacks, night-flying and other mysteries, to the virtual exclusion of all other mental activity. The unfortunate end to the story was that just before the six weeks elapsed I was summoned before the Group Captain who gave me the ' good news ' that the Air Ministry had reversed its decision and I was at liberty to sit my Bar Finals. Since I would have had absolutely no chance of passing them by then, I declined this offer and returned to my crew-room; I hope the Group Captain did not think me ungrateful.

So I remain to this day, like the legendary Babu, ' failed Barrister at Law ' —or perhaps more accurately ' not attempted '.

Our course at this airfield was a peculiar one, consisting of a number of fairly mature people, some even approaching middle age; a solicitor or two, a barrister (properly qualified this time), a publican, some company directors and so on. We were all reservists of some sort, by the quirks of the Reserve Organisation some being officers and some sergeants. The instructional staff at the Station, whose experience in the past had largely been in handling very young and humble acting pilot officers, were for a while thoroughly confused by our arrival and behaviour. Attempts to drill us on the parade ground or to march us to our flights were a dismal failure and were rapidly abandoned, although while they lasted they attracted audiences that far outnumbered those at comparable ENSA entertainments. However, a certain degree of mutual admiration and respect between staff and trainees soon developed and there were well attested examples of one of the latter offering the former lifts to the flight line or instructional block in his Rolls-Royce.

In a short while we were ready to pass to the operational conversion units which immediately preceded active service on squadrons. We were invited (perhaps only as a matter of form) to express our preference for operational role. With one dissenting voice we elected for fighters. The one dissenting voice was of course that of Leonard Cheshire, who had already attracted some raised eyebrows by volunteering for active service in the short-lived defence of Finland against the Soviet hordes.

'What are you up to now?' I asked him. 'Why do you always have to be the lone wolf?'

'Ah!' he said, 'that's the whole point. There are 19 of you. There'll only be one of me. They'll soon notice me'.

And they did. Within a year he had won his first DSO.

Very few of us in fact were posted to fighters, among the exceptions being Sergeant Denis Crowley-Milling, who made a great name for himself soon afterwards and retired as an Air Marshal. I was sent with two or three others to learn the art of Army Co-operation at Old Sarum. Here it was soon apparent that the dust of World War I still lay heavily over the whole establishment. We practised spotting the fall of shot, the observer passing the vital information laboriously by Morse key; we diligently interpreted messages transmitted to us by the display of white panels on the ground; at low speed and low altitude we conducted prolonged visual reconnaissance of a notional and remarkably acquiescent enemy; we flew 'line-overlap' photographic sorties involving prolonged and potentially suicidal flights at rigidly unvarying heights, speed and headings; and, God save us, we practised MPU—Message Picking Up by means of a hook suspended from the fuselage (as used in naval aircraft to engaged arrester wires on deck) which caught a rope cumbrously elevated between two poles by unenthusiastic soldiery; in ground school we did much the same things, the 'sand-table' representing the countryside on days unsuitable for flying. Artillery fire and other military explosions and conflagrations were simulated by a junior NCO, concealed under the curtained table, who blew cigarette smoke up through the surface at appointed times and places. His cigarette consumption was reputed to be over 100 a day, and, as he received these gratis as a training aid, the job was much sought after. Fortunately the association of cigarette smoking and lung cancer had not then been established, otherwise volunteers might have been harder to find.

Our training ambled along (as did our Hector biplanes) at a leisurely pace and in a totally unrealistic atmosphere. Two incidents from that time remain indelibly etched in my memory.

One of the ground instructors was a venerable and respected gentleman, whom I will call Major Smith. His subject was the Identification of Enemy Troops and Weapons and he displayed to us magic-lantern slides of this topic. On one occasion the subject was a light wheeled artillery piece, drawn by two German horsemen immaculately attired even to the classic spiked Prussian helmets. A member of the audience enquired whether the

13

Germans had not in fact mechanized any of their guns, with tracks or other means of self-propulsion.

' No, no ', said the good Major, ' they are very short of petrol you see '. We relaxed, reassured. The blitz and the panzers lurked comfortably over the horizon, a mere four months or so away.

The second occasion was when the already well publicized fighter pilot, Cobber Kane, visited us from France to instruct us on appropriate evasive action for the Lysander, which we were to fly, when intercepted by a Messerschmitt 109, ' Low and slow and turn inside him ' was the burden of his advice.

One of us asked him, perhaps understandably, what would be the difference if one were attacked by two or more Messerschmitts?

' Most unlikely ', replied the great man, ' they're pretty short of aircraft, you know '.

The unfortunate questioner was last seen, a few months later, being chased round a French church steeple by no fewer than 12 German fighters. One wonders whether in his final moments he gave any thought to this sage counsel.

However, at least we survived our period of instruction; converted to the Lysander; and in most cases reported shortly to our squadrons in France, where the ' phoney war ' still followed its uneventful course.

3　The Blooding

With three other tyros I was posted to No 13 Army Co-operation Squadron, one of four such units based in France in support of the British Expeditionary Force. The squadron's history went back uninterrupted to the earliest days of military flying and we were proud and fortunate (as we thought) to be posted to it. The squadron was stationed in North East France at Douai. On arrival we were told that there was little activity (though we noticed an aircraft with a couple of bullet holes through its rudder); and that we should proceed to the Officers' Mess and settle in, reporting to the Flights the next day.

The Mess proved to be located in a comfortable suburban mansion. There were very few people about and after a leisurely lunch I repaired to the patio to enjoy an unseasonably warm afternoon. Also enjoying the sunshine was a solitary Army major, reading a newspaper over a glass of port. Realizing my responsibilities as an officer and a host, I introduced myself, engaged him in conversation, offered him another drink (which he declined) and regaled him with some instructive anecdotes on army co-operation flying, the prospects of military activity and other matters of what should have been common interest. He appeared unappreciative, not to say taciturn and shortly took his leave, with some show of impatience.

The next day I reported for duty and was duly wheeled into A Flight Commander's office. After a long minute, he looked up and fixed me with a cold stare.

' We've met ', he said.

It was my Major chum of the day before. Nobody had explained to me that a large proportion of the Squadron officers were seconded from the Army. Another unfortunate initiation.

The routine of the ' phoney war ' was not demanding. I use the descriptive phrase then in common usage. For us in France it was indeed very largely ' phoney ' but it is too often forgotten that for a considerable proportion of the RAF even the earlier months of the war were periods of intense activity and valuable but too often bitter experience. The crews of the leaflet dropping Whitley and Hampden bombers, battling through ice and snow with unreliable engines and inadequate navigational aids, and of the unescorted Wellington bombers attempting vainly to penetrate swarms of Messerschmitts to attack coastal targets by daylight, would not have welcomed or indeed recognized the description. They were proving and disproving the basic doctrines by which air warfare had to be fought; but far too few of them lived through those first few months to practise themselves the lessons they had learnt. The manner in which the RAF's profes-

15

sional manpower, so strenuously and intensively restored and trained in the short prewar years, was frittered away before that war had even started for most of the participants was tragic, criminally tragic; but nobody ever seems to have admitted responsibility for the mistakes made or been penalized in any way for them. Reputations survived even when aircrews did not.

Our own lull was not to last for long. While it did we enjoyed our professional pursuits and various other less professional ones, notably in the Palais Oriental in Rheims, a centre of entertainment offering a notable variety of activities in an even more notable variety of scenarios.

Hitler, however, soon decided to put a stop to all this sort of nonsense, and the RAF in France was soon as tightly and agonizingly racked as its comrades elsewhere. The Lysander proved a robust and reliable fighting aeroplane but totally inadequate in performance and invariably heavily outnumbered; also the tactics and practices we had learnt at Old Sarum proved murderously unrealistic; enemy anti-aircraft fire and fighters demonstrated this, but at a dreadful cost. Even so our losses were less dramatically crippling than those of our fellow squadrons equipped with the Fairey Battle light bomber. At the time of its design in the early thirties it was one of the earlier monoplanes, a precursor of the Hurricane and Spitfire; it was widely acclaimed and put into extensive squadron service with the RAF (and also the Belgian Air Force). But by the time it was called on for use it was sadly outmoded, too slow and clumsy to evade enemy anti-aircraft fire and fighters, and too lightly armed to have any hope of beating off the latter. These defects, together with the deterioration in the allied ground situation which demanded its use in what amounted to suicide missions, led to shocking casualties, sometimes reaching 100 per cent of the aircraft launched against a particular target. The courage of the crews was superb but it was the courage of the doomed and the desperate.

This was brought home to me very sharply one day. I had landed at a Battle Wing airfield south of Rheims. During my short stay there, a new Battle flew in from England to replace one of yesterday's casualties. The pilot joined the circuit and made his approach but failed to lower his wheels. The aircraft crashed on its belly in a cloud of dust and the chastened pilot stepped out unhurt but due for at least a severe official rebuke from the Wing Commander for his carelessness. No doubt he received one; but to my surprise he was more or less fêted by the other aircrew. I soon realized why; his accidental destruction of the aircraft had prevented the inevitable loss to enemy action of the crew that would have flown it the next day.

The twin-engined Blenheim bombers fared little better. They were faster and somewhat better armed than the Battle but were called on to penetrate far deeper into enemy dominated airspace; and their fate was inexorably the same. So too for our Lysanders. Their performance, though highly publicized before the war, was inadequate and the tasks they were set were impossible. After quite a short period of fighting, my own squadron had lost all its serviceable aircraft; and those of us who survived joined the pathetic rabble of refugees fleeing westwards across France before the German armoured thrusts, constantly harassed and lacerated by enemy air

16

attacks. These latter seemed to us to be almost entirely unopposed, although here we made the same mistake as our soldiers later made at Dunkirk. Our fighters were indeed meeting the enemy and although heavily outnumbered, were blunting many of his attacks. But the air fighting was rightly conducted as far forward (that is eastward) as possible, to intercept the German aircraft before they could reach their targets. So we witnessed very little air fighting and wrongly deduced that there was none. We were tired and frightened, we misunderstood the realities and became embittered; so too at Dunkirk our men were tired, frightened, misunderstanding and embittered. 'Where was the RAF at Dunkirk?'

Nevertheless, although our fighters were doing their utmost, their numbers and inexperience and the total lack of any form of ground control rendered them comparatively ineffective. The enemy aircraft got through, to the sad detriment of our ground forces and of the vast helpless mass of refugees, among whom we could now unhappily include ourselves.

One particular aspect of this time that remains in the memory is how ignorant we all were, or were kept, of the general situation. All that we knew was that our own squadron had taken a disastrous hammering; that a major German offensive had been launched; and that in our sector at least it had met with considerable success. The fact that our army and that of the French had suffered an overwhelming defeat which meant that final victory, if it ever came to us, must be many years ahead remained quite unknown to us, certainly to the more junior; and I strongly suspect that our seniors knew little more. As a result, when finally many days later and after the main retreat through Dunkirk we reached England, we all fully expected to be re-equipped (with better aircraft, we hoped—there were always rumours of new Wonderbirds) and to return to France to carry on the fight. Only after we got home did we learn that that home itself was threatened.

Our squadron's retreating convoy initially consisted of 12 vehicles, including unbelievably the Chance Light. This was a large, heavy sort of lighthouse on wheels used to provide night illumination on undeveloped airstrips. It was by now quite useless since we had no longer any aircraft and was indeed a heavy and clumsy nuisance; but it was serviceable, no authority had been given to abandon it, so along it had to come. Fortunately some sensible driver ditched it quite early on and we were left with ten 3-ton trucks and a staff car. Even so the clogged roads, crowded with desperate and indeed often hostile pedestrian refugees and frequently under enemy air attack, made our progress painfully slow and often non-existent.

One of these air attacks provided an interesting illustration of the force of fear, panic, call it what you will. I was riding in the front of one of the lorries with a fellow officer called Payne ('Twinge' to his friends since he was quite small). High above and in front of us in the cloudless sky appeared a flight of fighter aircraft.

'Thank God, some Hurricanes at last—about bloody time too', said Twinge.

I agreed; but unhappily our aircraft recognition was not what it should have been and in a few moments the Messerschmitts that they actually were dived on our road and began strafing its packed mass of vehicles, animals and humans with their machine guns.

'Come on, Twinge, let's get out of here', I shouted, and we leapt out of the driver's cab, through a hedge and into a dense wood through which we were lucky enough to be passing. The trees were old and their trunks broad and tough and offered ample protection against machine-gun bullets, providing one could assess from which direction the fire was coming.

After a while the enemy withdrew and we were free to return to our trucks, which had remained unscathed. After a short distance we came again to the hedge through which we had shot so hurriedly a few minutes before. It was about four foot high, two foot solidly thick and consisted largely of thorn; and there were no gaps. Yet we had gone through it like hot knives through butter, as a glance at our tattered clothes and scratched limbs confirmed. We had to walk a good hundred yards before we could find a gate. Truly, fear lends wings to our feet.

In every man's life there are one or two turning points, looking back on which he can see that his whole future was determined by what decision he made or how events turned out. One of these occurred to me a few days later.

By now our convoy of vehicles was more or less on its own. The great mass of refugees was fleeing South and West, whereas we as it turned out were heading north-west for the coast at Cherbourg. The pursuing Germans, however, had not left us, their aim also being to reach the coast and close the trap on what was left of our forces. Sometimes they were so close on our heels that we could hear the rumbling of their armour behind us and to our flanks. I don't suppose we were their particular objective, but we certainly felt as if we were.

Because most of us were pretty vague as to our whereabouts and destination and because we were traversing totally unknown country, a practice developed by which whenever our straggling convoy reached a point of navigational decision, a major crossroad or a Y-fork, an officer in the leading vehicle would get out and direct the remainder in the right way. On this occasion the job fell to me. A typically long straight French road divided into two further long straight stretches, heading northerly and southerly. I was to steer our trucks up the former. I dutifully counted them as they passed; one, two, three . . . seven, eight, nine. Waving number nine on its way, I turned casually to look down the road for number ten, the last. The road stretched endlessly away from me, empty of all traffic or movement. My casualness turned to anxiety and then fear (only later did I learn that the last truck had been shot up and abandoned, and our vehicles now numbered only nine). Panic-stricken I started running, shouting, along the road, vainly trying to overhaul the last of the other rapidly disappearing trucks.

Of the dozen or so exhausted airmen in the back, one was awake. He saw me and called to the driver. 'Hold it a minute—look's like there's an officer running after us'.

They held it a minute. I arrived puffing and blowing and hauled myself aboard, and we were on our way again. I have always had a very soft spot for that airman and the driver, but for whom I would almost certainly have languished for five years as a prisoner of war. The driver, incidentally, was an officer, now a well decorated Air Marshal called Freddie Ball. He remains not only a good friend but a close neighbour; I sometimes let him buy me a drink for old time's sake.

By now most of our movement was in the trucks. Earlier on they had been loaded with a vast amount of now useless equipment to support aircraft already destroyed; and a great deal of foot-slogging had consequently been involved. This proved very tiring for men unused to such exercise; and the heat and the bitter, jostling crowds had made the going even harder. The equipment had, by the turning of some sensible blind eyes, gradually diminished until there was room on the vehicles for all the men. Food was a problem, however. We were supposed to be victualled for the journey but it was proving to be far longer than expected and we were getting very hungry. As a rule we were trying to avoid main roads where we were so vulnerable to enemy reconnaissance and consequent attack; and so missed most of the towns that lay on our general route. One evening a friend of mine and I decided on a little self-help. We walked into a village reasonably close to our camp in the woods and managed to buy some cheese, butter and eggs. However, on returning with our prizes, we were given a salutary and well deserved dressing-down by the adjutant for disclosing the position of the squadron (to whom?) and for selfishness in thinking of ourselves only when our men were hungry; we were duly abashed and handed over our purchases. However, the point of the lesson was to some extent weakened when that evening we observed our seniors tucking heartily into some splendid omelettes, whose provenance was not hard to imagine.

Our journey was taking us gradually north and west, and our final destination proved to be Cherbourg. Astonishingly, since the fighting at Dunkirk was at its peak, it presented a scene of peacetime normality, other than a general lack of activity in the harbour. Alongside a quay was a neat and smart cross-channel steamer, for all the world like a normal day-tripper's delight. She was to take home ourselves and some other unfortunates with whom we had met up in the last few miles. Whether her timely presence was a coincidence or a superb piece of organisation in the midst of chaos we never knew. But there she was and she took us home over calm seas under empty skies.

There was one final touch of farce. In addition to our splendid ship we found in the port, to our great delight, a NAAFI store and warehouse, fully stocked as the main depot for our troops in France. Hungrily we poured in and sought sustenance. The manager, immaculately garbed in his white coat of office, eyed these ragamuffins with suspicion and distaste.

' Got your ration cards, have you? '

' Cards? Of course we haven't. We've been on the road for weeks, man.'

' Sorry then. No cards, no issues. Those are my instructions and I have no authority to vary them.'

After a bitter argument and some threatening recrimination he finally melted to the extent that we were all conceded a single packet of cigarettes and one bar of chocolate; but we had to sign individually for them. I have no doubt that a day or so later the Germans took the rest with pleasure and gratitude; I only hope they took the manager too.

So a chapter closed; but there was a postscript that may be worth relating. On our arrival in England there seemed to be no plans for our next employment. Some of us were taken in at the RAF station at Odiham in Hampshire, since this was also a base for army co-operation squadrons. One of these was even still equipped with biplanes, the Hawker Hector, a development of the earlier Hart. There proved to be an atmosphere of great drama and tension. This squadron had been briefed for a dawn supply drop to the remnants of the Rifle Brigade still gallantly holding out in the citadel at Calais. The Germans encircled them with thousands of troops and guns; the French skies were completely dominated by the Luftwaffe; it was obviously going to be a suicide mission from which there would be no return.

The atmosphere was that of a Hollywood movie, *Dawn Patrol* perhaps, but this was real life and the fears and tensions were real. Some drank, Some wrote last letters or their Wills; officers were giving away their cars, their golf-clubs and even in some cases the secrets of their concealed passions for fellow-officers' wives. Confession and forgiveness were the order of the day. Upper lips were stiff and handclasps firm.

Before dawn the squadron lined up for take-off in an even more dramatic ambience. Sad quiet groups of families ringed the airfield. Last embraces were exchanged, the pilots emplaned and disappeared into the approaching dawn.

Unfortunately (or fortunately whichever way you look at it) they all got back, save for one who force-landed safely on the cliffs at Dover. The German defences had been caught napping. Their fighter defence was not yet properly organized and was ineffective at low level; their anti-aircraft guns, deceived by the incredibly low speed of the aircraft, missed, firing ahead of the targets for a change, other flak always seemed to be behind.

The denouement at base was remarkable, the unscrambling of yesterday's affairs proving a most complicated and embarrassing process. Confessions were retracted, not always convincingly; forgiveness was withdrawn and hostility substituted; divorce suits were threatened; personal possessions were sought for retrieval, not always successfully; and bargains struck were dissolved amid much contention.

We ourselves rejoined our squadron, re-equipped with a fresh batch of Lysanders and embarked on coastal reconnaissance against potential intruders and precursors of the invasion which by everyone, from the highest to the lowest, was accepted to be imminent.

For me at any rate it may now indeed be said to have taken place. In early 1974, by then an Air Marshal, I was invited by Richard Cox of the *Sunday Telegraph* to take part in a large scale computerized war game which simulated that invasion and attempted to assess its outcome. My colleagues were Rear Admiral Teddy Gueritz and Major General Glyn Gilbert. Our opponents were Admiral Ruge, who would in real life have been responsible for the minesweeping for ' Sea-Lion ', as the invasion was to be codenamed; General von Treppner, the potential commander of the air borne Wehrmacht force; and Adolf Galland, the very much real life Luftwaffe fighter leader. Large staffs of earnest bearded military experts assembled and theoretical battle was joined.

Perhaps surprisingly, in view of the outcome of the Battle of Britain and our vast naval superiority, the notional invading forces effected a successful landing on a wide front; and even more surprisingly were then soundly defeated, presumably by Dad's Army. In fact they had underestimated the difficulties of cross-channel maintenance of large forces, the same difficulties that faced our own Overlord invasion four years later.

' What did you say the speed of advance of your tug-towed barges was? ' politely enquired Teddy Gueritz of Admiral Ruge. ' Four knots? Yes, yes, that should have ensured an eventual landing—but perhaps disappointingly back on the French coast since the tide setting against you would have been running at five knots '.

So on paper we won that paper battle—but I could not resist a sneaking feeling of relief that they never actually tried it.

4 The Real Thing

As we were told with the highest authority at the time, the battle of France was over, the battle of Britain was about to begin. Naturally we wanted to play an active and more effective part in the latter than we had in the former; in consequence, without disloyalty to 13 Squadron, we wanted to leave the Lysanders behind us and join Fighter Command. This could not happen overnight, however, in spite of the crying need for fighter pilots. The operational training station was too small and very short of aircraft when all were needed in the front line; Hurricane losses in France had been far heavier than was advanced at the time.

We reformed 13 Squadron at Hooton Park in Cheshire, where, by coincidence, I had first seen the light of day, my wounded father having been at the time adjutant of the Cheshire regiment. By further coincidence we shortly moved across the river to Speke airfield which had been built on land originally belonging to my family home, Speke Hall. We conscientiously reconnoitred the South Western Coasts for the inevitable invasion and its precursing agents and saboteurs—necessary work, no doubt, but unexciting. Nevertheless not many aircraft were engaged on this task at one time and the remainder could be observed by the good citizens of Liverpool standing about somewhat uselessly on the airfield. After German bombers began to appear and the sirens to sound, this phenomenon naturally attracted some adverse local comment. Little purpose would have been served by trying to explain that the Lysander had neither the armament nor the performance to contribute anything to air defence—it still did not look good. As a result, the powers-that-be decided that when the alarms sounded, we should take off in formation, clearly visible to the now admiring citizenry, apparently about to engage the enemy. In fact we proceeded westward expeditiously to a safe distance out over the Irish sea, only returning when our trusty wireless operators could tell us that all was safe once more. It may have done some good, but it certainly did not make us feel very proud.

My posting to fighters duly came through but not before a couple of alarming hiccups. There was a project to attack the enemy invaders in the shallows or on the beaches. Even the tiny Tiger Moth was to join in, as was the Blackburn Roc. I received posting notices to both forces; and felt much relief as each was cancelled, particularly the latter. The Roc, a development of the naval Skua, with a heavy and unwieldy gun-turret superimposed, had an all round performance which was poor even by the standards normally imposed on the unfortunate Fleet Air Arm. Reputedly it had a maximum speed of 142mph; a cruising speed of 140; and a stalling speed of 138; which must have made it an interesting aircraft to fly.

22

However, these threats were duly lifted, and I was soon delighted to find myself learning to fly the robust and effective Hurricane at Aston Down. To some extent the Hurricane was the Cinderella of the Battle of Britain. Everyone has heard of the Spitfire and accepts it as the victor in that battle. This may have been due to its greater aesthetic beauty and finer aerodynamic form, or perhaps its admittedly higher performance. Films like *The First of the Few* by implication make it the forerunner of its type. In fact, the Hurricane preceded it both in design and in entry into service; and during the actual Battle about twice as many Hurricanes as Spitfires participated—indeed the Hurricane alone had borne the brunt of our air defence over France. Perhaps Cinderella is the wrong metaphor since the Spitfire was certainly not an ugly sister; but certainly the two were very much a partnership in the victory, the superior quality of the Spitfire being matched by the greater quantity of the Hurricane squadrons.

Having girded oneself for the battle and appropriately stiffened up the spiritual sinews, it was disappointing to be posted after the short conversion course to a squadron in Scotland. Nevertheless this was a very wise policy. Both sides paid dearly for flinging fledgling pilots with a handful of flying hours on fighters into the thick of it. Whenever it was possible—and too often it was not—our new boys were posted for a few weeks of essential experience to squadrons which, often after a heavy hammering, had been pulled back to a less active area. This made military sense, but the second-line squadrons themselves naturally resented being used as mere forcing grounds for those more heavily engaged; and squadron morale suffered from the fact that the main ambition of every pilot on the squadron strength was to get off it.

There was an amusing incident over this particular posting. Together with two other retreads from Army Co-operation I duly booked into Number One Hundred and Eleven Squadron at Drem on the South side of the Firth of Forth. The squadron authorities seemed surprised to see us but things were generally in a pretty good muddle, so we were accepted, given accommodation and put on the training programme. Within a day or so, plaintive signals were in circulation from Number Three Squadron, asking if anyone had seen or heard anything of Flying Officer Foxley-Norris and two other errant pilots assigned to them but absent on parade. It was the classic muddle between the Roman Figure III and the Arabic 111. We went on our way to our intended destination the other side of Edinburgh.

With this squadron we shifted about up and down the Scottish coast as the operational situation developed, from Turnhouse to Montrose to Castletown, close to John o' Groats, where we were supposed to contribute to the defence of the Fleet at Scapa Flow. We accumulated some valuable flying practice and even occasionally chased an enemy raider; but the warning and control system was rudimentary and only the most optimistic of us entered any claims for the few bursts we aimed at a fleeting Ju88 or Dornier.

Although we felt underemployed and out of things, life at Castletown was not without consolation. The weather and the countryside were lovely; rationing of such essentials as eggs and whisky had not penetrated so far north; and above all we were blessed in having as our station commander one of the legendary RAF twins, David Atcherley. Apart from the great professional value of his fighting spirit, his operational experience and his enormous enthusiasm, he ensured that life off duty was never dull.

He was under a minor official cloud at the time—something trifling to do with having hired and furnished a French chateau at vast expense as an Officers' Mess for his Wing a day or so before the Germans took it over free of charge—but this certainly did not dampen his spirits or inspire him to any undue conformity. The airfield at Castletown was under further development, including an extensive concrete perimeter track. The contractors, not knowing their man, were ill-advised enough to leave overnight a number of small steam-rollers employed to do the levelling work. The aircrew were equipped for personal locomotion with pedal bicycles, issued on signature by a hawk-eyed stores NCO. It did not take David long to discover that the maximum speed of the bicycles was approximately double that of the steam engines. What more natural then than to organize races between A and B Flights and between squadrons, one circuit engine-mounted to count against two à la bicyclette. Considerable excitement and fun, as dear Stanley Holloway would have put it, resulted; but also some notable tears and recriminations when burst boilers halted work on the airfield and burst tyres turned the stores section into a breakers' yard.

This exercise, however, was a mere aperitif for David's chef d'oeuvre. He learnt, with natural sympathy, that a storm beaten naval vessel had gone ashore near John o'Groats Head and after heavy pounding on the rock below, had become a total loss. Aerial reconnaissance, however, indicated the survival of a gun of considerable calibre installed on the vessel's stern. An intrepid climbing party with appropriate cutting gear was despatched; and before long, the otherwise almost non-existent ground-to-air defences of RAF Castletown were complemented by the same gun, supplied with what ammunition could be salvaged. Unfortunately, although it was designed to move both in the vertical and the horizontal planes, the latter capability was eliminated by its now being mounted in concrete outside the Station HQ.

Daylight was almost continuous in those latitudes and of a late evening David would lead parties of apprentice artillery men from the Mess to practise discharging this formidable piece. Its new and over rigid emplacement had regrettably left it pointing directly at the local lighthouse; the occupants of which displayed considerable alarm and despondency if one failed to apply maximum elevation to the gun during such exercises. Unhappily, David subsequently overplayed his hand by indenting to the Admiralty for a fresh supply of ammunition when the first batch was exhausted. In a matter of days a band of indignant matelots arrived to retrieve their weapon; and RAF Castletown once again lay wide open to enemy air attack.

There was intensive demand for pilots to replace the killed, the wounded and the exhausted; and, although we were still pitifully inexperienced in the role, we were soon sent south. Whether by good luck or by good manage-

24

ment, I was posted to Northolt to 615 Squadron, the auxiliary unit I had planned to join in 1939. Auxiliary squadrons enjoyed the privilege of having Honorary Air Commodores; ours was Winston himself and as ' Churchill's own ' we enjoyed a certain amount of limelight.

There were some expert and well tried pilots on the squadron. We were well led and we needed it for we were a mixed bunch, of varied and usually inadequate skills. Like many squadrons, we were sent a number of foreign pilots, in our case some Czechs and quite a large proportion of French.

Typically the latter were very much individuals. Many of them had escaped by their own initiative from the French Desert Air Force (one learnt with fascination that, during their lonely tours of duty in remote North African stations, their personal and officially supplied equipment had included full-sized inflatable rubber ladies, a sound precaution no doubt against undesirable local involvements, homosexuality or cafard). Of the half dozen Frenchmen on the squadron, the one to make the greatest name for himself later was Rene Mouchotte, handsome, charming and debonair but a most courageous and determined fighter; he was eventually killed leading the Biggin Hill Wing. The only survivor among them was Henri Lafont, now one of the brains behind the Paris Air Show.

I was bitterly disappointed but should perhaps not have been surprised to find that my personal success on fighters was not much better than on Lysanders. Indeed success is quite the wrong word—by the time I left Fighter Command after eight or nine months I had inflicted no confirmed damage on the enemy and had cost the country two Hurricanes; one crashed overshooting at West Malling after a battle; one shot down in flames from which I parachuted from a great height, landing near Ashridge in Kent and enjoying the quite common experience at the time of being identified by the intrepid locals as a German. On recovering from a heavy and painful landing, I was surprised to be almost frog-marched away at the point of a pitchfork; only when a police car turned up and the driver was told ' Got one of the bastards here for you ', did I appreciate the lie of the land and dispel the misunderstanding with some hauteur.

The frequency of such incidents was not surprising. The greater proportion of those descending by parachute were in fact German; and by the time our propaganda machine had got to work on that proportion, it was quite natural for the good people of South East England to presume that a downed pilot was a Luftwaffe pilot. Whether any of them ever learned to recognize Al Deere after he had baled out eight or nine times I cannot say. Perhaps the worst recorded case was that of Flight Lieutenant Nicholson, who baling out badly burnt after the epic fight that won him his Victoria Cross, was duly shot by a member of the Home Guard as he descended.

My failure to distinguish myself in the Battle was by no means as uncommon as many people would imagine. Particularly, one's shooting was haphazard and untutored, most of us having been thrown into the Battle quite without adequate training in that highly scientific art. We did not often get into an attacking position and when we did, we missed, firing at too long ranges and without enough deflection. Those who survived eventually learnt by experience; but in 1940 the successes went to the few old hands, the naturally gifted and the lucky. It is a statistical fact that on both sides more than three-quarters of the aircraft destroyed were shot down by less than a third of the pilots.

At least we weaker brethren with non-existent or even minus scores had no cause to search our consciences when the postwar publication of actual German losses indicated that some exaggeration had been made in those claimed.

In November we moved further south from Northolt to Kenley, which had been the peacetime base of 615 Squadron, so it was something of a home-coming and we were made duly welcome. Sadly though, only one of the original Auxiliary pilots, Tony Eyre, was with us by then. By no means all had been lost in battle but the original strength had faded away under various pressures and demands. The ground crew, however, were still largely the original men. This was one of the attractions and indeed strengths of the auxiliary squadrons. The continuity of service of the airmen and NCOs and the cohesion of local ties and origins added a depth to their dedication and a drive to their diligence which was unequalled in any other unit; I was to experience this again much later in the war. Although the eventual disbandment of the Auxiliary Air Force may have been based on sound military and economic arguments, the loss of this special relationship inflicted an irreparable blow on the RAF as a whole.

By November, the Battle of Britain as historically defined was over; the attempts by the Luftwaffe to break the back and spirit of Fighter Command, so as to obtain air superiority to cover a sea-borne invasion, had been defeated. History indicates that this was the enemy's intention, although how close he ever came to implementing it is less clear. By now certainly the idea had been abandoned for the winter of 1940/41; and it seems probable that already Hitler had already determined to divert his main attack toward the East. The weight of the air offensive was switched to night bombing, aimed to cripple our industrial production and destroy morale. Against these tactics our Hurricanes were of very limited use. They were designed to conduct daylight defence under visual conditions; and in darkness or even cloud or bad visibility were quite ineffective. Various ingenious methods of overcoming their deficiencies in this respect were attempted, including the use of a pair of aircraft, one carrying a powerful illuminating 'Turbine' light and one armed; but these came later and were never very successful. In the winter of 1940/41 we patrolled diligently when the moon or our searchlights could help; but sadly our casualties to our own guns and balloons exceeded those we inflicted on the enemy. It was a hazardous and discouraging business at which only a few developed much skill.

To supplement the heavy raids by night, the Germans mounted numerous daylight fighter sweeps, a proportion of the aircraft carrying externally slung bombs. The latter reduced the Messerschmitts' performance considerably and made them fairly easy meat if you could catch them still loaded; but customarily they regained their speed and manoeuvrability by jettisoning their bombs haphazardly when threatened. The top cover and the high level sweeps were conducted now exclusively by Me109s, the clumsier twin-engined 110s having been relegated to the night role with the conventional bombers. Furthermore, these aircraft were of the latest breed, the Me109E and F which were superior in many respects to the Hurricane Mark II we were now receiving. They were faster and had a greater ceiling; our assets were our manoeuvrability, the help of our ground control system, and the fact that we did not have to conserve fuel for a long haul back to base.

Engagements were thus fairly evenly matched, as were the casualty rates. We had to contest the freedom of our skies but there seemed to be a lot of flying done for little result; and, consequently, the limelight that had flooded our efforts earlier eased off somewhat. In this connection I repeat what I said before about the Battle of France. In spite of the glare of publicity, the radio bulletins, the newspaper headlines, and the political speeches not many of us realized quite how important the victory had been, or quite how narrow its margin. For the average squadron pilot, it was just a question of flying day after day, hoping to survive and hoping to inflict damage on the intruding enemy. We did our job as best we could with varying degrees of success; but at the time I do not recall thinking that one was making history.

At about this time our morale was much lifted by the permission given us to go over to the offensive on a small scale. Nothing is more frustrating or exhausting than to be kept continually on the defensive: it is like trying to play tennis when the other man is always serving. It is a sound principle of war that the initiative must be grasped and held whenever the opportunity, however limited, arises.

Our initial offensive moves took two forms; 'Rhubarbs' and, later, 'Circuses'. The Circus, which developed fully only after I had left Fighter Command, followed more or less the pattern shown us by the Germans, consisting of either a small force of bombers heavily escorted by fighters attacking a choice of targets sharply limited by our range; or offensive fighter sweeps over enemy-held territory; or, frequently, a combination of both. The Rhubarb was a bad weather, poor visibility operation in which a very small force of fighters slipped across the Channel under cloud cover and attacked opportunity targets such as military rail, road or canal traffic, installations—or even on one memorable occasion, a large ceremonial parade.

In January 1941, 615 was given its first crack at a Rhubarb. There was much enthusiasm and competition. The Squadron Commander decided to lead a pair himself, and I was nominated to act as 'weaver', ie to cover the vulnerable tails of the attacking aircraft on the way over and back. The weather was suitably bad, a lot of broken cloud with some snow storms blanketing both coasts. The idea was to fly over just above the cloud, find a suitable hole through which to let down, and attack any opportunity target we found. We took off, climbed above the lowest layer of cloud and were on our way. Flight Lieutenant Foxley-Norris 'wove' like mad, concentrating solely on his defensive role. We seemed to be flying for a long while, with a number of changes of course. At last our leader appeared to spot the gap he was looking for and with a hand signal (we had kept radio silence until then) led us down to almost ground level. I moved up into the No 3 position to join the attack.

We were over typical farm and downland; visibility was poor and it was snowing; suddenly I spotted the masts and installation of an RDF (later Radar) Station. Switching my gun button to ' fire ', I called the attention of the others to this juicy target. There was an agonized bellow from the leader, ' That's Pevensey, you clod '.

We had apparently crossed the Channel, found no holes in the cloud cover, and returned to our own coasts to feel our way home. Nobody had told the diligent weaver. A lot of airmen, and indeed WAAFs, had a lucky escape—assuming of course that I had managed to hit the target for a change. It was quite an easy one.

Rhubarbs became a popular sport but they proved surprisingly expensive. The enemy's detection system was improving and his anti-aircraft fire was effective against low-level targets; since it was known that we could only reach a few, they were often heavily defended. We wondered if the game was worth the candle, balancing losses against damage inflicted. The authorities apparently decided that it was; and I have no doubt, harking back to my observations about the offensive and the initiative, that they were right.

I have probably written enough about this period. It has been well covered by other participants and by historians; also by fiction writers; and by makers of cinema films. Some of the latter were appalling; anachronistic, melodramatic and inaccurate. Others, like *The Battle of Britain* were creditably precise historically and went far to capture the real spirit of the times; but in one respect it, and many other companion pieces, conflict with my admittedly faulty memory. Everybody is made to look so earnest and gloomy.

Now, my recollection is that one was indeed often very depressed and pessimistic on occasion; for much of the time very frightened indeed, either of what was happening or of what one expected to happen tomorrow; but for the rest, we had a hell of a good time. We had, by contemporary standards, enough to eat; by any standards, plenty to drink. We were given time off when we could be spared. And many people were only waiting to entertain, both publicly and privately, the heroes of the hour. It didn't matter whether you were personally a hero or not. The light blue uniform, the wings and the ostentatiously undone top tunic-button of the fighter pilot were a passport to any party. We were not inclined to forego such offerings; there may have been, in fact was, something of the ' Eat, drink and be merry, for tomorrow we die ' spirit about it all but, if anything, that added edge to one's enjoyment and to one's determination to get the last ounce out of life while it lasted. This sounds melodramatic but is true.

So there was a lot of gaiety to life, sometimes a little forced and shallow perhaps, but none the less real. We did not always gloom, philosophize or despond; we frequently caroused. In my judgment the best attempt to portray and recapture the atmosphere is to be found in H. E. Bates' story *A Moment in Time*.

For me the end came undramatically. After a long period in the front line, in March 1941 615 Squadron was to be pulled back to a quite area, North Wales. The opportunity was taken to reassign some of the experienced pilots and post in younger and fresher ones for further training up to full operational standard. I was one of the former and was to go to the Central Flying School for a short wartime course to learn to be an instructor. I protested strongly, and I believe honestly; but to no avail. We had our farewell parties and left Fighter Command—in my case not to return for 15 years. It was never quite the same again.

Even later on in the War, the flavour and atmosphere of Fighter Command underwent a subtle change. It became perhaps more professional. The hectic urgency of 1940 was no longer there. The dangers were just as great and the enemy just as threatening; but the day of the casual, nonchalant amateur—the Max Aitkens, Cocky Dundases and Laddy Lucases—was past. It was succeeded, laudably no doubt, by the day of the efficient killers like Johnny Johnson and Ray Harries; but never again would there be incidents like that in France in 1940 when a highly competent and confident Luftwaffe major on learning the circumstances of his final combat with an auxiliary flown Gladiator, exploded in fury (but perfect English), ' I just don't believe it—shot down by a bloody barrister in a bloody biplane! '

Wars are not won by amateurs but battles sometimes are. In saying this I do not of course suggest that everyone who flew in 1940's Fighter Command was an auxiliary, or a reservist like myself; but many of them were and they lent a certain yeast to the steadier mass of regulars. Perhaps I may illustrate this by what is certainly an exaggerated, if not a fictitious, anecdote. A regular officer commanding an auxiliary squadron had quite rightly banned the practice of a ' victory roll ' after a combat; too many valuable pilots had lost their lives attempting one, unaware of structural damage to their own aircraft. He was therefore justifiably indignant to observe one of his aircraft inverted at low level over the middle of the airfield before coming in to a smooth landing. The carpeted pilot was all innocence: ' Victory roll, Sir? Me, Sir? Certainly not—it was just that I'd dropped my cigarette holder on the cockpit floor and it seemed the easiest way to retrieve it. Didn't want it gumming up the works for the next chap, naturally '.

5 Out of the Line

In developing and teaching the techniques of flying instruction, the British had been pioneers and were now acknowledged masters. The credit for this lay basically with the Central Flying School at Upavon in Wiltshire. Certain individuals had of course played large parts in establishing its standards and maintaining them throughout periods of economies; but the institution itself, with its traditions and its professional pride was the keystone of the arch.

At the time I was in no mood to appreciate this. I was disappointed to be leaving my squadron and to be taken off operational flying when I had accomplished little except personal survival. I was tired and strung up, and had not sufficient insight or maturity to judge correctly the merits and value of the Central Flying School. To me it seemed a backwater, full of people who took themselves unduly seriously when the serious affairs of war were going on elsewhere. The discipline was strict and old-fashioned. The shibboleths and conventions appeared out of place in the middle of a world war, as indeed they were.

I will quote one example of what I mean. As a Flight Lieutenant I was quite senior among those at Upavon, outranking many of the instructors; and was indeed the senior pupil on my course. The Officers' Mess was a fine old-fashioned building with large public rooms and traditional service. I noted, in all innocence, that one of the main ante-rooms seemed less crowded than the other. Consequently one day, wishing to read a newspaper quietly, I took my post-lunch coffee into the former and occupied an armchair. On my appearance, there was a marked hush and the atmosphere chilled by several degrees. I sat on in peaceful ignorance of my dreadful gaffe. I had not only entered, horibile dictu, the sanctuary of the Instructors' Room; I had actually seated myself in the Chief Instructor's Chair! Only H. M. Bateman could have done justice to the appalling scene. My reputation for brash insolence was established forever. The fact that nobody had bothered to tell us humble students about this vital fact of life was held to be neither here nor there. One should have known.

At the end of a very abbreviated course, I qualified as a flying instructor, Category B1 (A Categories were quite rightly not awarded from these short wartime courses); nevertheless I had an awkward moment in my final graduating tests. I had worked hard at my aerobatics, my instrument flying and my practice forced landings, and was confident of my ability to instruct others in them and to satisfy the examiner accordingly. Once airborne, his voice came briskly over the communicating tube.

' Right—I am a brand new pupil. Give me the patter for straight and level flight '.

30

I had never been taught it. ' Straight and level flight, Sir? Well, er, you fly the aircraft—er—straight and keep the wings and the—er—longitudinal axis—er—as level as possible. That's more or less it '.

I was rebuked and corrected; but the rest of my performance apparently satisfied the great man. I was given my category; and duly reported for final interview to Group Captain ' Speedy ' Holmes, a great air force figure of his day, well liked and respected. Nevertheless an unpleasant few minutes followed for myself.

' Well, Foxley-Norris, I am glad to see you have passed out creditably. But in general I have been thoroughly dissatisfied and disappointed by your performance. As senior pupil you have not set the sort of standard we expect here. You have been casual in your manner and carefree in your general approach. You made it clear from the start that you did not want to come here ' (this was true enough), ' and did not appreciate the privilege of doing so. You have set a poor example to younger and more junior students. I shall report accordingly on your personal papers. Dismissed '.

I ' dismissed ', crestfallen but somewhat resentful. I had been sent to Upavon to become an instructor. I had become one—and quite a good one. What more did they want me to do—sprout wings and a halo?

It should all have been very transient but there was to be a somewhat ironic sequel.

Two or three years later, Speedy Holmes had been promoted Air Vice Marshal and was commanding a Group in Flying Training Command. One of his stations was RAF Montrose in Scotland and here the Wing Commander, Chief Flying Instructor, was unfortunately killed in a flying accident. To provide a replacement, the Air Ministry proposed to promote a Squadron Leader Foxley-Norris, and consulted the AOC as to whether this would be acceptable. The AOC, who apparently had a good memory, made it emphatically clear that it would be totally unacceptable; further, that he would not have ' that bloody man ' on any of his Stations.

Very unhappy—and perhaps unhappiest of all for my unlucky brother, who happened to be the Squadron Leader Foxley-Norris the Air Ministry had in mind, and who consequently forfeited a well-earned acting rank.

Having a brother in the Service is often quite useful. Whenever anything creditable happens, one is quick to claim responsibility; discreditable incidents can be promptly disowned as cases of mistaken identity. The Atcherley brothers were of course the acknowledged masters in this field. On one occasion in 1943, David Atcherley was flying home from North Africa for an important operational conference. The weather over Southern England was very bad, and he had to be diverted to the only airfield that was still open, Portreath in Cornwall. As was, and remains mandatory during flying, an ambulance and a fire tender were standing by the Air Traffic Control Tower. David, now going to be very late for his meeting, taxied in at break-neck speed, leapt out of the aircraft and into the ambulance whose engine was running, and disappeared in a cloud of dust toward the nearest main line railway station, Redruth.

The Station Commander was naturally furious. He addressed an indignant letter to Group HQ. It passed up the line to Command and to Air Ministry. The letter despatched a stern rebuke in writing to Air Commodore Atcherley; but unfortunately it was addressed in error to the other twin. Batchy hastened to reply:

Sir,

I have the honour to acknowledge your letter of 23 November, whose sentiments I entirely endorse. To remove, without authority or permission, the emergency ambulance from an operational station, thus hampering the flying programme and imperilling the lives of crews already airborne is quite unforgiveable; and fully merits the tone and content of your communication.

I have to inform you, however, that I personally was in no way involved in this incident. I can only presume the officer concerned may have been my brother, Air Commodore D. Atcherley.

I have the honour to be, Sir,
Your obedient servant
etc etc

PS   Personally, I always take the fire engine on these occasions.

To return to my own circumstances, on leaving Upavon I went to instruct at RAF Ternhill. Almost immediately, however, I was struck with an acute appendicitis, was whipped into the nearby Cosford hospital and had the offending organ efficiently removed. I was lucky enough to be sent to the Palace Hotel, Torquay, to convalesce. This splendidly lavish Edwardian establishment had been taken over by the Royal Air Force for the medical rehabilitation and after care of officers. Its facilities, especially the swimming pool and the grounds, were ideally suited to the purpose. The great majority of my fellow inmates had been wounded in action. Among them were some who had suffered burns, although the worst burn cases were of course still in the hands of Sir Archibald MacIndoe at East Grinstead. This was my first direct encounter with this particularly horrible type of injury, although I suppose the fear of it had always been in the back of my mind. It made a most profound impression on me, as did the courage of the victims whose pain was continuous and whose disfigurement was often lasting.

Here once again the local hospitality was unbelievably lavish—and once again I felt an impostor as a recipient of it; but I soon gave up protesting, lay back and enjoyed it. My honest attempts to explain that I was actually only recovering from a minor and routine bit of surgery were greeted with disbelief by the local doubting Thomasinas:

' Oh, go on, you're all so modest, I'll bet it was something terribly exciting and dangerous, only you're not allowed to tell me about it '.

Even the eventual exposure of my humble scar did not always prove convincing.

My recovery was all too rapid, but before I was ready to leave I learned that I was only to return to Ternhill to pick up my goods and chattels, and was then to proceed to point X to take ship for country Y to join the Commonwealth Air Training Scheme.

32

This scheme was a most ambitious project, brainchild of some of the more long-sighted staff in the Air Ministry. It was based on the fact that large sections of the Empire, although admittedly far flung, enjoyed skies entirely free of enemy aircraft and indeed largely free of any aircraft; and territory with ample space for building and operating airfields. Canada and Rhodesia were selected as the two main elements of the scheme and development was rapid. There were a few drawbacks, for example the length and comparative hazard of the journey by sea; and the fact that the clear weather and flying conditions were very different from the fog, smog and blackout that the newly trained aircrew had to master on their return home; but the advantages of the scheme far outweighed any such drawbacks and it paid handsome dividends in thousands of strong, fit, well trained young aircrew. The tragedy, of course, was that so many of them lasted so short a time on operations before death, wounding, or capture; but this was one of the harsh realities of World War II, harshest perhaps overall in Bomber Command but applicable more or less throughout the RAF and indeed all other air forces. Losses, though hushed up at the time, were terribly heavy. They may be illustrated by a recent disclosure arising from a major programme in Holland to reclaim much of the remaining area of the Zuyder Zee. A special aspect of this programme, most conscientiously pursued by our Netherlands friends, was the historical research into and identification of the British bomber aircraft which lie beneath the surface of the Zuyder Zee. It is authoritatively estimated that they number about 700: 700 aircraft, perhaps 3,000 human beings, in one comparatively small inland sea. Those of us who helped to train those human beings can never free our minds of such appalling figures.

On arriving at Port X, we embarked on the good ship *Pasteur*, a French liner which operated before the war on the transatlantic run. Although we did not discover this until later, she was still on that run, which produced the admirable bonus that being regularly stored and victualled in peacebound America, the standard of eating and drinking was unchanged since her halcyon days. Being young and healthy, we stared with astonished appreciation at the menus for five-course breakfasts and seven-course dinners, and fell too with a will; and of course paid the penalty. Even young and healthy digestions cannot withstand a sudden switch from nearly two years of wartime austerity to such Lucullan fare; however, we soon recovered, except for the chronically seasick. My friend Peter Barnes was heard to complain after he had bade farewell to his lunch, ' I wouldn't mind so much if it was the same old spam, but Paté de Foie Gras aux Truffes à la mode de Madère—this is really tragic '.

Being a fast ship, the *Pasteur* proceeded unescorted. This was standard practice for the large speedy liners. It was felt that to confine them to a normal convoy of perhaps 12 knots maximum transit speed deprived them of their greatest asset and prospect of survival. So they crossed alone at maximum cruising speed, relying on zig-zagging and continuous course changes to outpace and outmanoeuvre any U-boat. High speed demands high propeller revolutions and the *Pasteur* was consequently rather a noisy ship. So it was with some relief that on about the sixth morning we woke up to find the engines stopped. Presuming we had reached our destination, we hurried up on deck to determine where it might be.

We had reached no destination. We had suffered a major mechanical breakdown. We were alone and stationary on a calm sea under a cloudless sky with what appeared to our anxious eyes to be unlimited visibility. We lay there, helpless, immobile and entirely unprotected, for nine hours. They were perhaps the nine longest hours any of us had spent. By the grace of God (I use the phrase in its strictest sense) our presence and our plight went unobserved. Towards dusk our reluctant engines sprang into life again and we resumed our passage.

Two evenings later we did in fact reach our destination, which turned out to be Halifax, Nova Scotia, thus establishing at least that our new home-from-home was likely to be in Canada. It was apparently going to be Penhold, a brand new base (it proved to be so new that it was unfinished) equidistant between Calgary and Edmonton in the Western province of Alberta. The idea was that most of the instructors were to fly the aircraft across; the remainder would proceed by a splendid Canadian Pacific Railways train which, because it travelled day and night, would cover the journey as quickly as the aircraft which had to make refuelling and crew-rest stops on the way.

I was one of those selected to fly and accompanied the chief instructor and some of my fellows to the nearest airfield where our aircraft, newly uncrated and assembled, awaited us. They proved to be Airspeed Oxfords, which in turn meant that they were twin-engined. I had never flown a twin-engined aircraft in my life. I informed the CI of this unfortunate fact. He was incredulous at first, but eventually agreed that a trans-Canada flight, involving a proportion of night flying, was perhaps not the ideal form of first-solo on type. I returned somewhat ignominiously to the train and was replaced by someone more appropriately experienced.

On arrival, we found Penhold to be typical of all newly constructed airfields. A lot of bare earth, mud and contractors' debris; a couple of runways; and all the multiplicity of buildings and accommodation required to operate a large flying training school and house its staff and pupils. Everything was on an austere scale (there were no resources to waste even in western Canada), notably the food, which was a nasty come down after the *Pasteur* and the CPR. Beer was rationed and spirits unobtainable on the base. But we had a job to do (I myself naturally had to do a quick conversion on to the Oxford aircraft, with such arcane mysteries as asymmetric flying and so on); and soon our first batch of pupils arrived and we got down to it in earnest.

Training courses were kept as short as possible and as much ground and air instruction was crammed into them as could be. It was difficult to balance the requirements of quantity against quality under the production line pressures of war. A high rejection rate was understandably unpopular with the authorities, and as a result it must be admitted that a number of marginal cases were allowed to graduate. This was a situation by no means

34

unique to the British. All air forces showed a steady deterioration in aircrew capability as the war progressed, although the Americans coming in later and with a vast field of selection probably suffered least; more and more of the experienced men were killed, or had to be taken out of the line and their places filled by younger, rawer boys whose enthusiasm and courage were unquestionable but whose expertise did not always match previous standards.

The same applied to the instructors, which did not help matters. Through no fault of their own, and certainly rarely through any choice of their own, many of those sent to instructional duty had seen no active service. They were selected as they graduated from their own flying training, sent on a quick CFS course and became 'instant instructors'. Consequently they often initially lacked the maturity and experience which help to make a good instructor, and frequently suffered from inferiority complexes into the bargain. The point may be illustrated by the fact that I, with not much more than 500 hours flying in my own log-book, was one of the most experienced pilots on the original staff at Penhold.

When we were not working we explored the local countryside and got to know the people. Both could be described as rugged but attractive. The local town, Red Deer, was then only an overgrown village and the people were mostly farmers and small traders. Although basically reserved and shy of strangers, when one had made friends they proved hospitable and generous. One slight acquaintance expressed concern to hear that when we had a weekend off we went to Calgary or Edmonton by bus; and thereafter insisted on lending us his almost new De Soto saloon for these expeditions. There were many similar incidents.

It was interesting to meet and talk with a type of human being almost unknown to us previously. Their geographical remoteness and frequent personal isolation on outlying farms in the vast prairie produced a perhaps self-centred and narrow outlook, but also bred self-reliance and strength of character; and native wit and shrewdness supplemented what was sometimes an inadequate educational background. Sometimes—but not always, as I learnt on one particular occasion.

One of our Oxfords had crashed into a stand of timber close to a remote farmstead, killing both instructor and student. I was ordered to conduct the formal enquiry and by good fortune found an eyewitness in the person of the farmer's wife, a strong, quiet, pioneer type of middle-aged woman, who had seen the whole affair. I was trying to establish whether the aircraft had gone in out of control or whether the pilot had been attempting a wheels-up forced landing, due perhaps to engine failure.

' Now, Mrs Jurgeson, as I understand it, you saw the aircraft flying almost directly towards you. If you can picture the shape of the wing, did it look to you as if the rear half was sort of bent down?'

' I don't get you.'

' Just think of the wing as you saw it. Did the part furthest from you appear to be lower than the front part?'

' I'm sorry—I just don't get you.'

' Oh, dear! Well then, if you imagine the wing as a single plank of wood, did the further side of it look as if it was hinged downward? '

' Oh! *Now* I get you. Did he have his flaps down? No, I'm pretty sure he didn't.'

My legal training should have taught me not to underestimate the intelligence of a witness! Incomplete though it had been it did result in my being in some demand as a defending officer at Courts Martial; and this in turn once again brought me in conflict with authority.

A senior NCO had been caught in flagrante delicto misusing service petrol in his own car. I defended him, but the evidence was overwhelming and he was convicted. I observed, however, that legally the charge had been wrongly framed and was bad in law. I advised him to appeal. His appeal was successful; and his conviction was quashed. I was then sent for by the Station Commander and given the most almighty dressing-down for being responsible for a ' known criminal ' getting off scot-free, to the general detriment of good order and discipline. When I referred to a lawyer's prime duty to his client, I was told that I was not a lawyer but a serving officer; as such my prime and only duty was to my Service; and that in ignoring this I had shown myself thoroughly disloyal to that Service. I was not entirely convinced; but he had four stripes and I had only two, which adds much weight to any argument.

After a few months, I became due for a short period of leave and, with a couple of friends, visited Spokane, Seattle and British Columbia. We were much struck by the wonderful scenery of the latter and its comparative sophistication after the lone prairie; among other places, we visited the superbly sited Operational Conversion Unit at Patricia Bay, where pilots were being trained on my old love, the Hurricane. It seemed a very happy and enviable place.

It was therefore with genuine enthusiasm that, on return to Penhold, I found a notice on the crew-room board stating that the standard of experience on these Operational Conversion Units was proving inadequate; that all pilots who had completed an operational tour should be employed on them rather than at Flying Training Schools; and that applications were invited from qualified people for transfer. My name went down immediately and I sat back and waited for my posting to the desirable Patricia Bay, British Columbia.

Never volunteer. I was sent instead to the highly undesirable Debert, Nova Scotia. Nestling among the mud flats and mosquitoes at the top of the Bay of Fundy, this insalubrious resort had the coarse but well merited nickname of ' The Pile on the Arsehole of Canada '. On arrival there, I noted a row of Lysanders and a large number of Lockheed Hudson twin-engined maritime reconnaissance-bombers. I reported to the Chief Instructor, who as usual was not expecting me.

' Foxley-Norris, eh? They haven't told us anything about you. What are you here for? '

' I'm not sure, Sir, but I imagine to fly the Lysander. I've got quite a lot of experience on them.'

36

'No, no—it can't be that. The Lysanders belong to the local Royal Canadian Air Force Squadron. You must be a Hudson instructor.'

And such, willy nilly, I became, picking up the art of the thing at the same time as I taught it. The aircraft was much faster than the Oxford and much more sophisticatedly equipped, eg with an automatic pilot. As a flying machine it was comfortable and not too difficult; but on landing and take-off it had a tendency to swing violently off the runway into the mud. When this happened, one of the undercarriage legs usually came up through the wing, where the main fuel tanks were stored and which was itself partly made of magnesium. The resulting conflagration was intense, instantaneous and usually lethal. The swing could only be cured by coarse use of the rudder bar and violent application of the hand brake which was located between the student's seat (left) and the instructor's (right).

A reliable method of differentiating between students and instructors off-duty was thus established. A student's right hand normally bore scars on the top; these resulted when he got his hand to the brake first and the instructor's finger-nails descended on it an instant later. For the instructors, it was the left hand that suffered in the same way.

Debert was a pretty dreary place. The weather was generally bad and the visibility worse. It was reputed that in winter the fog from the Bay of Fundy normally restricted visibility to a few hundred yards at most; in the summer the clouds of mosquitoes had the same effect. Local entertainment was restricted by the fact that Nova Scotia was a 'dry state'. A few officers, who tended to be older and more senior than those at the Flying Training Schools, had their wives and families with them and did their best to provide some sort of social background; and indeed the instructional staff were an amusing and entertaining lot. Nearly all had performed arduous tours of operations on Hudson squadrons before coming to Canada, and formed a closely knit group of friends which initially we newcomers had difficulty in penetrating.

The liquor laws in this dry state had one interesting side effect. A ration of 'hard liquor' could be obtained at the Government liquor stores; and issues were sufficiently scarce that most purchasers liked to have a quick couple of swigs from the bottle straightaway. These same laws, however, imposed very heavy penalties on a driver found with an opened bottle of spirits in his car. The solution was obvious. The local worthies obtained their bottle, sat down on the steps of the liquor store, lowered its entire contents and then attempted to drive home. The law thus more or less guaranteed that a given proportion of drivers were drunk in charge of their cars. The restricted pub-opening hours in Australia, with the consequent frenzied 'five o'clock swill', produced much the same effect.

We worked hard at Debert, with the occasional short leave during which I had my first encounter with New York under the able and expert guidance of 'Ginger' Weir (later Air Vice Marshal and one of the most popular men in the Air Force). In under a year, during what was supposed to be an 'operational rest', I pounded in 500 hours flying in and around the circuit of Debert. At the beginning of 1943, a posting notice arrived. Squadron

Leader Foxley-Norris to Ferry Command to transport Hudsons across the Atlantic. I mentioned mildly that I had scarcely ever flown out of sight of land and my navigation was rudimentary. ' Ah ', they said, ' but you have 500 hours experience on Hudsons. Get on with it '.

So I got on with it.

Ferry Command's operations were based at Dorval, near Montreal; and at least one had the privilege of residence in that delightful and highly entertaining city. After a little specialized instruction in the art of beam flying and so on, I clambered into a Hudson and pointed it Eastwards, accompanied by a navigator and a radio operator, both NCOs. The rest of the fuselage was filled with a large special fuel tank to give the necessary added range. Even with this, one normally had to make a number of intermediate refuelling stops at Goose Bay in Labrador, at Bluie West One in Greenland or at Reykjavik in Iceland; wind and weather determined how many one had to use before eventual arrival at Prestwick.

On my first arrival there, my two NCOs thanked me most effusively. I was a little surprised.

' Why all the gratitude, gentlemen? '

' Well, sir, we were really relying on you. It was our first trip across, you see.'

I did not like to enlighten them.

Two other incidents stay in my mind of that time. On one occasion we squeezed in as co-pilot an American Air Force Major assigned to the UK on special duty. After our arrival, he too thanked me but this time for the chestful of medals to which he had just become entitled. If my memory serves, they were the Overseas Service ribbon; the Combat area ribbon; the 1943 Active Service Star; and last but not least the Arctic medal (we had refuelled in Greenland en route). If I had crashed on landing he would have had the Purple Heart too—I felt quite apologetic.

One evening before take-off from Montreal, an RAF Padre approached me in the Mess and enquired if I was returning to the UK; and if so, could I take Flight Lieutenant Niven back with me?

' No, I'm sorry, Padre, we don't take passengers on these trips.'

' No, no, you misunderstand; he's not really a passenger in that sense, you see.' And he produced a small square lead-lined casket, in which apparently lay the ashes of the unfortunate Niven, lately killed in a flying accident in Canada. 1 agreed somewhat reluctantly, but only after I had insisted on receiving precise instructions on how to dispose of my somewhat macabre supercargo in the UK.

On arrival at Prestwick, I was interrogated as usual as to the contents of my flight-bag, which contained only my personal effects, a bottle of whisky, some cigarettes, a few pairs of nylons, and of course Flight Lieutenant Niven.

' What's that? ', queries the Customs Officer suspiciously. I explained the circumstances.

' Right ', he said, ' open him up."

' I'm damned if I will ', I replied.

' OK; if you won't, I will '. And he did, sifting the powdered ashes thoroughly before resealing the box.   Noting my astonishment and disgust, he explained:

' Not to worry, Sir, you seem to be an innocent party.   You see these little caskets being lead lined, are impervious to X-rays.   Consequently, they've become a pretty popular way of smuggling industrial diamonds into the country recently; we've found several well-seeded '.

Flight Lieutenant Niven and I went on our way to London.   His eventual destination was straight out of Evelyn Waugh.   The particular department of the Air Ministry that dealt in such matters was eventually run to earth in an upper storey of what had been (and still was in part) Drage's Furniture Store in Oxford Street.   Entering a small outer office, the good Niven firmly under my arm, I was greeted with the vision of a WAAF of almost unbelievable beauty, languor and refinement.   She asked me what she could do for me.   I refrained from giving a factual answer but introduced Niven.

' Ah, yes! ' she said, ' do put him down somewhere, there's a darling. Had a good trip, did you?   Bless you, how you boys do get about, don't you? '

I hesitated.

' Er—I was told I should get this receipt signed by an officer.'

' Were you now?—well, how fussy can they get.'   She pushed open an inner door with a long, silken leg (no grey lisle stockings for her).

' Charles, be a dear and sign something for this man, will you—are you signing things today?   I forgot to ask.'

A silver-haired, bustling gentleman dressed up as a Wing Commander but clearly intrinsically of the theatrical profession joined us from the inner sanctum.

' Ah, customers, eh?   Busy, busy, busy—it's all action here you know, my dear boy.   Now, who have we here?   Niven, eh?   Not dear David, I do hope—no, of course he's with the other lot, isn't he?   Well, well, let's see.   Have you got the N file there, Angela?   Newcombe, Newson, Niles— ah! here he is, poor chap.   Niven, Q. G.—dear me, *what* a long time he's been coming.   Never mind, not his fault, I've no doubt.   Well, there's your little slip of paper signed, dear lad—delighted to see you again any time— although, of course, perhaps not *too* often, ha! ha!   Goodbye then, goodbye —Angela, say goodbye, dear.   That's it then.   I shouldn't take the lift, it usually gets stuck.'

I found myself out in the street, still disbelieving.   I hope Niven, Q. G., got a laugh out of it anyway.

I was due to return to operational flying, I hoped, and my time in Canada had come to an end.   I looked back on it with mixed feelings.   I had made a lot of new friends and visited a lot of new places, including several trips to the United States.   There was much to enjoy and much to be grateful for, although the ' operational rest ' I was supposed to be on scarcely justified the name.   One point was a matter for regret.   Not unnaturally, the Commonwealth Training Scheme had to be content with what geography was left after the needs of the Royal Canadian Air Force had been met; and not unnaturally the latter chose the best places for themselves.   Consequently the great majority of the RAF stations were either remote outposts in the scorching/freezing prairie (Penhold had been one of the best) or mudholes in the damp forests of the East Coast.

Thousands of young men, of whom at least hundreds survive to this day, saw this and only this during their wartime spell in Canada. As a result, there are a large number of middle-aged men in Britain today who have a quite unbalanced picture of what Canada is really like and a basically unfavourable impression. Inevitable perhaps, and perhaps not very important—but a pity nevertheless.

Like most of them, I was glad to be going home. I could not help wondering what changes to expect. News was, as we all know, much subject to optimistic propaganda, often amounting to falsification (on the day I had been first shot down together with two others of my flight the official bulletin reported that we had lost no aircraft to enemy action). The Dieppe débâcle, with its heavy toll of Canadian lives, had naturally made considerable local impact, but apart from that, little bad news was allowed to filter across the Atlantic and the good news was greatly exaggerated. For example Alamein and the victory in the Western Desert had been trumpeted all over the newspapers, radio and cinema screens; whereas the setbacks and sharp local defeats in Operation Torch at the opposite end of the Mediterranean were much played down and, if mentioned at all, blamed on unseasonable weather. An unfortunate consequence was that those crossing the Atlantic eastwards to fight for the first time, whether Canadian-trained pilots or American GI's, left with a quite unwarranted euphoria. I remember seeing a fellow-officer at Debert reading the account of the thousand bomber raid over Cologne with a pretty glum face.

'What's up, Winkle? It all sounds pretty good, doesn't it?'

'That's what worries me, Christopher. I'm afraid at this rate it will all be over before you and I get back and have a chance of another go.'

It wasn't.

6 Once More into the Breach

The problem of my next appointment was somewhat complicated. My operational experience was on Lysanders and Hurricanes, and I suppose I was pigeonholed somewhere as a fighter-pilot. On the other hand, by now my greatest amount of flying hours was on the twin-engined Hudson, operational only in Coastal Command. The deduction I made from this was that I would be best employed on twin-engined fighters in Coastal Command, ie Beaufighters (the Mosquito was only just reaching Coastal Command). Contrary to the form book, that was more or less what I got; that is to say I was indeed posted on to Coastal Beaufighters but they were in fact largely employed in attacks on ships. ' Never mind ', I thought, ' bigger targets to hit '.

This sounds light hearted, but does not really reflect my mental attitude at the time. When I had come off operations in the Spring of 1941, I had become underconfident and thoroughly frightened. In my heart, I had to admit doubts of what I would make of another operational tour and whether I had the guts to face one, especially now that as a Squadron Leader the responsibilities of leadership would be added. I could only hope for the best and do some fervent praying.

As it turned out, all was well. I remained frightened, as nearly all operational pilots were at one time or another and to a greater or lesser extent; but I never found my fears overwhelming, and was able to overcome them without too much difficulty—to my slight surprise and great relief. On reflection, I think there were two reasons for this.

In the first place, I suppose what I and most people in my circumstances really feared was being hurt—wounded, crippled, disfigured and especially burned. Flying at maximum ceiling of well over 30,000ft in the Hurricane one could never really dispel the thought of how long it would take to come down in flames (' But they, they will not blazing fall, ten thousand feet to die '). The Coastal Strike wings by contrast flew very low, usually below 500ft, climbing only slightly to make the actual attack. The flak was nearly always very heavy and so were the casualties; but, if you were hit, you usually went straight into the sea and can have known very little about it, for at most a second or two. I came to the conclusion that death itself was less frightening than pain, certainly in my own case.

Secondly, the tactics we had to adopt more or less took the decision of whether to press home the attack out of one's own hands. We flew almost always in daylight, in large visually maintained formations. The leader of wing, squadron or flight was at the arrow head of a number of other aircraft. One could not have shirked or evaded an attack without it being quite clear to a lot of people that one was doing so. Many found the fear of shame more compelling than that of danger—perhaps I was one of them. Moral cowardice may be more telling than physical cowardice.

After a short conversion course I was posted to No 143 Squadron at Northcoates on the Lincolnshire Coast. The squadron with two others formed the Northcoates Strike Wing. Its operational task was to attack enemy coastal convoys and shipping at sea or often in harbour, usually off Holland but also off Germany and Belgium; the strategic concept was that it was anomalous for Bomber Command to put vast effort into destroying German land communications, if the alternative sea-lanes were left untouched. The weapons with which the attacks were made were cannons and rockets, both of which were fired in a shallow dive aimed directly at the target. It was a less lethal performance than the low-level bombing by Blenheims that had preceded it—but not much less.

Perhaps fortunately, the squadron was shortly detached from the Wing and sent south to Cornwall. Our main parent base was St Eval but we were further detached to Portreath, a small grass airfield north of Newquay on the coast. Our operational tasks here were twofold. As fighters we mounted constant patrols over the Bay of Biscay and the Western Approaches, to cover not only our merchant and naval ships but also to attempt to counter the activities of German fighter aircraft, which were giving our Liberator and Sunderland anti-submarine aircraft a bad time. Our secondary role, which occurred too rarely, was to intercept and attack lone enemy blockade-breaking ships, which tried to run the gauntlet to French ports with vital cargoes such as rubber or aluminium.

Much of the fighter work was rather tedious. The Beaufighter in the Coastal fit had an endurance of over five hours and during that time the pilot could not leave his seat. Encounters with enemy fighters, operating from the Brest peninsular, occurred more by luck than management, since neither their nor our radar covered our operational area at low level. When the enemy aircraft were Junkers 88s we did not have much to worry about; when they were Messerschmitt 109s or Focke Wulf 190s, we had a great deal.

It was the luck of the draw after all, and life was reasonably pleasant and carefree off-duty in Cornwall in the summer of 1943. Our squadron mess (most accommodation was away from the base for safety reasons) was in a little suntrap of a hotel on the cliffs, and there was plenty of beer and good local cider; but not, by now, of food. In the fourth year of the war rationing was beginning to press hard. We had an occasional special bonus, however. The Liberator crews used to land frequently at Gibraltar after a patrol; some victuals were more readily available there and, to show their gratitude for what we were at least trying to do for them, they promised on one occasion to bring us back not only a cask of sherry but an actual ham. We decided to give a party based on these delicacies, and, with the help of some extra butter scrounged from a helpful neighbouring farmer, sent out invitations to 'A Ham Sandwich Party'. We owed a great deal of hospitality locally and a fair crowd of people turned up. With the gramophone flat out and the sherry and cider flowing freely a really good old-fashioned party developed. The sun set romantically, the dancers bounced on the patio and the singers filled (or perhaps rather fouled) the Cornish night. At last a cry was raised, ' The sandwiches. What about the sandwiches? ' And there they were in the dining room, thick with butter and mustard and everything they should have been. It was a memorable party, as everyone agreed.

I was first down to breakfast early the next morning nevertheless, as I was due to fly. There on the sideboard lay a beautiful untouched ham. I questioned the mess sergeant.

' Did they give us two hams then, Sergeant Villiers? '

' Oh, no, Sir. Just the one—the one you see there, Sir.'

' But what about the sandwiches last night then? '

' Sandwiches, Sir? Nobody gave me any special instructions about them, Sir. They were just the usual Spam, with of course the extra butter.' Nobody had noticed. There must be a moral there somewhere, but I'm never quite sure what it is.

So life went well; but for me there was a notable cloud on the horizon—no bigger than a man's handwriting, as one might say.

In June, the Wing Commander CO took some leave and left me in temporary command of the squadron, which involved some desk-work. I was duly minding the desk one morning when the squadron adjutant entered.

' Good morning, Johnny, anything doing? '

' Nothing much, Sir; just one rather awkward letter about a security leak. Seems somebody on the squadron has been writing about things he shouldn't. I'll see if I can find out who it was.' He passed me the offending letter. It was addressed to a Flt Lt Hinks at RAF, Hendon; it gave a chatty account of the squadron's general activities; it was signed ' Chris '—in fact it was signed by myself.

What had happened was this. Hendon was the administrative base in the UK for Ferry Command. If one wanted to write to anyone serving in that command abroad, one addressed him at Hendon. Ferry pilots were normally transported back across the Atlantic after their delivery flights in Liberator bombers; and the mail for those in Canada was sent from Hendon in the same aircraft. Being internally addressed it of course passed through no censorship and no security checking.

That was the system when I was in Ferry Command and the officer I wrote to (who of course was fully security cleared himself) had been one of my recent associates there. But the system had changed. Letters so addressed were now being treated as overseas mail and accordingly censored; of this of course I was quite unaware. I decided to bite the bullet.

' I shouldn't bother to look much further, Johnny. I wrote it myself.'

' Oh, I see, Sir. Well, not to worry—but I'm afraid there'll have to be a summary of evidence just to keep them quiet.'

' Go ahead.'

The summary of evidence was duly taken, with a stony faced gentleman from the Special Investigation Branch in attendance. I explained how the misunderstanding had arisen and the mistake had been made. I pointed out also that the letter had been addressed to a fellow officer, and in any case only contained the broadest account of our operational activities, such as was regularly published in the newspapers. The summary was concluded and I thought no more about it.

Shortly afterwards the CO returned and it was my turn for a short leave. My brother was by then instructing at Cranwell and I decided to spend a few days with him and his wife. On the night of my arrival, there was a supper-dance in the Mess and in the middle of it a telephone-call came through for me. The squadron adjutant was on the other end of the line.

'Johnny here, Sir. I'm afraid you're recalled from leave immediately and posted to the main base at St Eval.'

'Really? Why on earth?

'Well, Sir, I don't know—but the Wing Commander Operations was killed there yesterday. I imagine you'll be taking his place; that'll be it.'

'I'm sorry to hear that—but I suppose it's an ill-wind. Will you send a plane to pick me up in the morning? Right—goodnight, see you tomorrow.'

I returned to the bar. Several people inquired ' what that was all about '. I told them that if they showed a bit more respect for the new Wing Commander, he might consider buying drinks all round. The party hotted up.

The next morning, with somewhat of a hangover, I flew back to Portreath. The off-duty squadron aircrew were in the bar.

'Hullo, Sir, what brings you back so soon?'

I explained matters and stood some more rounds of drinks in consequence. After lunch, I reported in to the Squadron CO to say goodbye.

'Well, Foxley, I'm very sorry to see you go—particularly under these circumstances.'

'What do you mean 'under these circumstances', Sir? Aren't I going to St Eval to be Wing Commander Operations?'

'No, no, nothing of the sort, I'm afraid. You're going there to be court-martialled.'

Quite a shock. I spent a busy period sending off a few signals, the gist of which amounted to ' for promotion, read court-martial throughout '; and proceeded to St Eval, where the next day I was duly charged with ' Breach of Security, in that . . .' and placed under open arrest. I retired to a neighbouring billet to suck my teeth and prepare my defence.

What had happened was this. I had committed a technical offence for which under normal circumstances, I would probably have been formally rebuked by my Commanding Officer. By unfortunate coincidence, a junior Canadian officer serving on one of the St Eval squadrons had written a letter home which was infinitely more indiscreet than my own, giving full details of time, location and names of recent casualties, which clearly could have been of considerable interest to the enemy had it fallen into his hands. This had been intercepted by the normal censorship. The writer had got away with a very severe official rebuke, but higher authority had taken a serious view. ' There's too much of this sort of thing going on. Make an example of the next offender, preferably a senior officer.'

Squadron Leader Foxley-Norris had walked right into it—up to his neck as usual.

I was fairly confident of the validity of my defence; but the weeks that passed before the case was heard accentuated one's worries; and there was a more fundamental worry too.

Court Martial law has one practical defect. Under normal process of law, the accused is assumed innocent unless and until proved guilty; and in theory of course that applies to court martial law as well. In practice, however, every serving officer knows that courts-martial, with their complicated procedure, their calls on the time of busy officers, details of organization and paper work, are an infernal nuisance, especially on an active operational station in wartime. Consequently, everyone leans over backwards to avoid having to convene one. As a result, there is inevitably at least a subconscious feeling among the officers sitting in judgment ' Let's face it, this chap wouldn't be standing there unless he'd done it.' I had considerable experience of courts-martial by now and was well aware of this phenomenon —which was not exactly comforting.

However, on the dreaded day, all went well; my chances were perhaps improved by an unexpected circumstance. By coincidence, another Squadron Leader from Portreath was now answering to the same charge, and his case was heard before mine. His offence appeared to be much more serious and indeed much more interesting to the members of the Court. He was a middle-aged man, a World War I pilot who was employed in the operations room, naturally a place holding much secret and important information. Having become rather fuddled at a Mess dance, he had proceeded to conduct not only his wife but also his mistress in succession all over the operations room and to explain just what went on there.

After this juicy case, the main feature of the programme as it were, in which the unfortunate man was convicted and heavily punished, my own must have seemed very dull stuff; and anyway it was getting on toward lunch time. The only testimony against me was in the written summary of evidence, and my defence of honest mistake and largely innocent material was readily accepted. I was acquitted.

Relieved, I hurried to a telephone and rang the squadron adjutant to give him the good news of my imminent return. There was an embarrassed pause.

' Well, Sir, it's rather awkward, I'm afraid. You see, when you—er— went away, they posted in a replacement to command your flight. I expect you'll be getting a posting somewhere else. I'm sorry, Sir.'

I returned to the Mess, now somewhat deflated and was invited to sit next to the recent President of the Court Martial, a Wing Commander, who addressed me cheerfully: ' Well, I expect you're feeling a pretty happy man right now, aren't you? '

' As a matter of fact, not altogether, Sir. I've just been told that through all this unfortunate business, I've lost my command.'

' Ah, well ', he replied, ' that'll teach you not to do it again, I hope.'

Considering he had just officially pronounced that I had not done it at all, it seemed rather an odd remark. I continued my lunch in silence.

My posting came through promptly, to No 252 Beaufighter Squadron in the Middle East; and to get there by the fastest possible means.

7 Mediterranean Interlude

The reason for the urgency was that the squadron, based in Cyprus, was heavily engaged in the ill-fated operation against Cos and Leros in the autumn of 1943. The background was as follows:

Turkey had remained neutral throughout the war, a fact for which I suppose we should be grateful, for she must have been sorely tempted on several occasions, eg after the German invasion of Greece and Crete or Rommel's apparently unstoppable drive through the Desert, to throw in her lot once more with her World War I ally. Now the tide of war had turned. The Germans had been driven out of Africa and Sicily and were being steadily pushed back in Italy. More importantly, their failure to score a quick victory in Russia indicated an inevitable eventual defeat there. It was felt by Churchill that a dramatic military stroke under the direct gaze of the Turks might persuade them to declare war against an apparently helpless Germany, thereby much improving the prospects of one of his pet hobby-horses, a Balkan thrust against the allegedly soft underbelly of Europe. The targets selected were the two large German-occupied Greek islands of Cos and Leros. They were to be taken by an amphibious coup de main, including paratroops, and held as a base for further attacks on the vulnerable German garrisons and communications in the Aegean.

Politically it may have been sound thinking, but militarily it was a non-sense. We, of all people, should by now have learnt the lesson that without local air superiority such an operation could not possibly succeed; and it did not need much military genius to appreciate that air superiority must lie with the enemy. He could operate high performance fighters continuously over the target islands and their approaches from Rhodes and Crete, which straddled the invasion route, and from the Greek mainland. Since Air Marshal Tedder firmly refused to divert any fighter aircraft from the Western Mediterranean for the purpose, all that we could pit against them were Beaufighters, operating from Cyprus at maximum range against defenders superior both in performance and numbers. The result was a foregone conclusion. We got a bloody nose and our unfortunate troops, whom we could not cover and the Navy could not resupply, were forced to surrender. It seemed unlikely that the watching Turks had been very impressed: certainly they did not rush to join us.

The air side of the operation had been conducted by the Middle East Air Force. Air Vice Marshal Saul was apparently made the scapegoat for a failure which was inevitable from the start; and was no more seen. One could not help wondering whether the consciences of his superiors were entirely clear over the casualties sustained and the share of the blame.

252 Squadron, like Achilles, retired to its tents. These particular tents were located by the banks of the Suez Canal and here we were re-trained in attacks with rockets, only then being introduced into the area. When we were not flying ourselves, we could sit on the Mess Verandah and watch with fascination the mine-sweeping of the Canal by special Wellington aircraft. The Germans had taken to dropping magnetic mines into the Canal by night. The Wellingtons were fitted with huge cartwheel devices under their fuselages. These emitted a magnetic discharge which detonated the mines. This sounds very simple but the selection of the right height at which to fly called for very nice calculation and precise flying. If the aircraft flew too high, the magnetic discharge was not strong enough to do the job; if too low the mine exploded and destroyed the aircraft. The pilots were phlegmatic men of reflective mein, who drank a great deal of beer. We admired them very much.

The operational role now given to 252 Squadron was to participate in the interruption of supplies to the German garrisons on the Aegean islands, in particular those on Crete and Rhodes. These garrisons had been established in 1941 after the enemy's successful invasion of the area. They constituted the means of suppression of our unfortunate Greek allies, and they also offered a serious air and sea threat on the northern flank of our own Mediter-ranean communications. For reinforcement and military supplies they depended on shipping or on the old three-engined Ju52 transport aircraft, the supply routes running from the mainland, usually Athens itself but also from Salonika and other smaller ports (the shorter the sea crossing the better, but even in harbour they had no guarantee of safety).

Our job was to try to starve the smaller garrisons into surrender, and to render the large ones operationally ineffective or at least eliminate their offensive capability. The difficulty arose of course that in starving the Germans we were likely also to starve the native Greeks. In attacking shipping it is usually impracticable to distinguish between those loaded with military stores and those carrying the ordinary necessities of life—with some exceptions of course such as fuel tankers. Sometimes we had intelligence information on cargoes and knew which were ammunition or troop carriers–but usually they were just ships and had to take their chances. Luckily some of the bigger islands were more or less self-supporting for food; and the rest were maintained by small sailing or powered caiques, which we left alone unless they shot at us. On one memorable occasion we encountered about dawn a 16-oared boat, which might have come straight out of Homer, its crew rowing like mad to make harbour before the light came; we wished them well but naturally they could not hear our ribald cries of ' Well rowed, Leander ', or ' Give her ten, Argonauts '.

Our own counterforce, as well as 252, included No 603 Beaufighter Squadron, two South African light bomber/reconnaissance squadrons, and a squadron of torpedo dropping Wellingtons for night work. Additionally of course the Royal Navy threatened the sea routes with the occasional submarine and with a varied force of small attack boats, dashingly com-manded in the family tradition by George Jellicoe. The leading British representative with the Greek resistance forces on the mainland was Monty Woodhouse. We had all been contemporaries at Winchester, which made things matey.

Unlike some of the better publicized Resistance movements in other occupied European countries, the Greeks never gave up their bitter and unrelenting campaign against their occupiers. Their coasts, islands and mountains formed admirable terrain for guerilla activities and only in the larger towns and more developed areas was there any considerable degree of collaboration. The fact that a great proportion of the resistance forces were Communist-infiltrated and finally Communist-dominated only reflected the higher standard of foresight and unscrupulous manipulation that existed in the Russian organization and policy staffs than our own. At least they fought and tied down numbers of German forces—which was all that mattered at the time. A German soldier guarding a railway in Thrace was not available to serve at Stalingrad or Caen.

The enemy's defences against our squadrons consisted of anti-aircraft guns on the ships and shore installations, special flak-ship escorts and the ubiquitous Messerschmitts on the larger islands; they also, unusually, included some Arado 196 seaplane fighters but these were too slow to worry us—indeed the boot was on the other foot and they tried to keep out of our way on most occasions. The Messerschmitts could outperform us, but could not pick us up on radar at our low operating height, and interceptions were mercifully rare.

We were ourselves stationed at various landing fields in the Western Desert, of which Mersa Matruh with its lagoon for sailing and swimming (it is now a holiday resort) was much the most attractive; Gambut, further to the west, was perhaps the least. Why we were moved so often when the land fighting was now so remote and the enemy air threat negligible, was difficult to understand; and it irritated the NCO's and airmen who were great hands at making purses out of sows' ears and could convert the dreariest bit of sandy scrub into a home-from-home, given time to put some roots down.

There is a lesson here for all who ever have to command troops, and particularly British troops. When you are compelled to mess them about, if humanly possible explain to them why. 'Their's not to reason why' is a military principle which has long lost its validity—if it ever had any.

On paper the lumbering Ju52s should have been easy meat and indeed one of my pilots shot down two on his first operational sortie. However, they were normally used at night and made skilful use of their very low speed. If they suspected we were after them, they flew at about 60 knots at below 100ft above sea level, which presented great difficulties to the Beaufighter. Our efforts proved discouragingly unsuccessful, partly due to the fact that being basically anti-shipping aircraft rather than specialist night fighters we were not equipped with Aircraft Interception radar. Our discouragement generated a classic instance of leadership by example.

We were being briefed one evening for a night of attempted aircraft interception around Crete. A light aircraft descended on our desert land

Above left: 'The car that started it all.'

Above: How I won my first medal;
Coronation, 1936. ('On your left, Your
Grace—Duchess on the right.')

Left: 'Who's started what war?'
3 September 1939.

Above left: 'Snow White and Assorted Dwarves.'   1939.   (Later Air Marshal Sir Christopher Hartely.)

Left: 'Poor man's Bloody Red Baron.'   CNF-N, 1939.

Above: 'Churchill's Own.'   615 Squadron Northolt, Autumn 1940.   [*Graphic Photo Union*

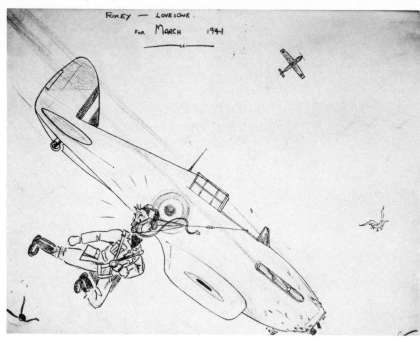

Above left: 'Pride goeth before…'

Left: '…a fall.'

Above: Lockheed Hudson. CNF-N, Debert, Canada, 1942. [*Crown Copyright*

Below: 'What a crude lot.' CNF-N, Debert, Canada, 1942.

Left: 252 Squadron Beaufighters over
desert, 1943.   [Crown Copyright

Above: 'Don't look now, Herman.'
[Crown Copyright

Right: 'Thar she blows!'   Attack off
Crete, 1944.   [Crown Copyright

Above left: Big bang off Rhodes, ammunition ship, 1944. *[Crown Copyright*

Left: 'Left hand down, *Herr Kapitän.*' German E-Boat crashing after attack, 1944. *[Crown Copyright*

Above: 'Going up Sir?' *[Crown Copyright*

Right: 'No, down I'm afraid.' Arado Ar196, 1944. *[Crown Copyright*

R.A.F. Form 96A
S.575A. (Naval)

MESSAGE FORM

Office Serial No.

Z337a/GHQP/3-43

Call and Preface	IN :— CUT	603 SQUADRON		No. of Groups	Office Date Stamp
				GR	

(Above this line is for Signals use only)

TO* 603 SQUADRON

FROM* AH QEM .

	Originator's Number	Date	Your/My	Number and Date
(Write horizontally)	P.160	17.10.	P11	24 . 18.10.

FOUR	BEAUFIGHTERS	ARE	TO	DEMONSTRATE	5
OVER	THE	TARGET	AREA.	FROM	10
1645	TO	1700	Oct 17.	AIRCRAFT	15
ARE	NOT	(REPEAT)	NOT	TO	20
OPEN	FIRE	BUT	ARE	TO	25
LEAVE	NO	DOUBT	IN	THE	30
MINDS	OF	THE	ENEMY	THAT	35
THEIR	FATE	IS	SEALED	IF	40
RESISTANCE	IS	CONTINUED.			45
					50
					55
					60

This Message must be sent AS WRITTEN and may be sent by W/T. Signature | This Message must be sent IN CYPHER and may NOT be sent by W/T. Signature | Originator's Instructions§ | Degree of Priority§ | TIME OF ORIGIN 1613 .

†Originator to insert "NOT" if message is not to go by W/T over any part of the route. (Below this line is for Signals use only.)

System In	Time In	Reader	Sender	System Out	Time Out	Reader	Sender	System Out	Time Out	Reader	Sender

T.O.R

T.H.I.

§The Signal Department is responsible that these details are transposed to the appropriate portion of the message form and that all possibility of compromising distinguishing signals, etc., by omitting to remove their signification from the address, etc., is avoided. Before delivery of the message these details are to be re-inserted in P/L.

Above: That signal.

Above right: Banff Wing returning from strike, January 1945.   *[Crown Copyright*

Right: Banff Wing Boss (Max Aitken).   *[Crown Copyright*

Left: 'It's not easy to attack ships downhill.'   *[Crown Copyright*

Above: 'Welcome home, lad.'   *[Crown Copyright*

Below: 'Self inflicted wound.'   *[Crown Copyright*

Above: 'The Hunter hunted.'   *[Crown Copyright*

Right: 'For you, the war is over.'   4 May 1945.   *[Crown Copyright*

Above: 'Still Churchill's Own.'   Battle of Britain Day, Biggin Hill, 1947.   *[Planet News Ltd*

Below: 'I hope this damn brake works.'   On honeymoon, St Moritz, 1948.

ground and out of it stepped Group Captain Max Aitken, by then the Senior Air Staff Officer of No 201 Group, our parent formation. He listened to the briefing (he was of course already a night fighter pilot of established repute); and then asked me if I could let him have an aircraft and observer so that he could join the programme. I naturally complied, and shortly after midnight he took off.

Four or five hours later he returned. He reported, as was confirmed by his observer, that having had no luck on the approach lanes to Crete, he had joined the actual circuit of the main German airfield at Heraklion, the most heavily defended point on the island. He had caught the enemy napping and had destroyed three enemy aircraft and damaged two. He completed his sortie report and departed. He had not lectured to us or rebuked us; he had merely shown that it could be done. He recommended his observer for a DFC.

I and the rest of us had learned a valuable and well-proven lesson—actions speak louder than words.

Our anti-shipping operations were predictably more effective. The Germans tried to complete their passages by night which gave some cover. Our Beaufighters were equipped with ASV (Air to Surface Vessel) radar but it was not really accurate enough for completely blind attacks, and we needed a helpful moonpath to give us a good chance of success. It was about this time that I was given another insight into the phenomenon of fear.

Formation attacks by night were obviously impractical; to try to concentrate the weight of attack, we adopted a so-called ' Daisy Chain ' tactic, a series of single aircraft conducting a West to East patrol across the Aegean to intersect all the enemy's north-south shipping routes. The aircraft were spaced at 10-minute intervals. If a pilot found a target, the others following behind or flying ahead could be directed on to it. This worked fairly well on several occasions; but one night one of the leading pilots sighted an enemy warship and called up the remainder, informing them of its location, course and speed, and that he was climbing to attack with rockets. As he did so, still transmitting, he must have been hit and set on fire. He screamed piercingly all the way down to the sea for perhaps 10 or 15 seconds. It was the most appalling sound any of us had ever heard. That night none of the other crews reported sighting or attacking that or any other ship.

Our daylight anti-shipping activities occasionally flared into major operations when reconnaissance or intelligence reports told us that the enemy had been driven to the comparatively desperate measure of sailing large daylight convoys; desperate, because he did not have adequate aircraft or warship resources to defend them effectively against concentrated attack. When we got at them, their losses were consequently high: but so were ours. On one major attack, our CO, Wing Commander Willie Meharg, who was leading the wing, was badly hit on his run in. His starboard engine became a flaming torch, he flicked over and went straight into the sea at high speed. Unhappily there was plenty of both eyewitness and photographic evidence of exactly what had happened. So, when I had the painful duty of breaking

49

the news to his wife, who was a Wren officer in Alexandria, I could not offer her any hope of his survival. She took it very bravely.

I was considerably embarrassed, although of course personally delighted, to hear a few weeks later that both Willie and his observer were prisoners of war, the only injury they had between them being some burns to the observer's exposed right arm. To this day, neither remembers anything until they found themselves safely floating in their Mae Wests amid the wreckage of the enemy convoy.

The severity of our losses was due to the inflexibility of the tactics imposed on us by our weapons, the rocket and the cannon. Both had to be fired in a shallow dive with the aircraft pointed at the target, ie directly down its gun-barrels; the maximum accurate range for the rockets was 800 yards and for the cannon considerably less. Furthermore, since the enemy's flak defences were naturally strongest at the beginning of our attack, it was the leading sections of our squadrons that suffered the most. Casualties were thus heavy both in quality and quantity; we could perhaps afford the former even less than the latter as time went by. Discussion was endless on how we could improve matters—particularly among those of us who were normally to be found in the front row.

I remember two solutions being attempted, neither with success. One was by a Squadron Commander who decided to lead from the back, ie leading the last instead of the first section of aircraft. There was no comparison with the Duke of Plaza Toro. He was a provenly brave man and nobody on his squadron doubted it. He merely reasoned that his survival was operationally important, and that from the more rearward position he could also apply more tactical flexibility to the attack, ie if the first sections had clearly lethally damaged the main target ship, he could switch the remainder to other targets. It worked very well for a time; but higher authority discovered what he was up to and disapproved. I thought they were wrong, and I still do.

Another imaginative and perhaps more acceptable solution to our difficulty was along these lines, ' If we have so many losses because both our aircraft and our weapons have to be pointed directly at heavily defended ships, why not modify the flight path of the weapons so that only they have to be so pointed? '. The idea was that the aircraft would fly at a safer distance parallel to the convoy and fire salvos of rockets which would themselves turn through 90° in mid-air and head for the target. This was to be accomplished by fitting the rocket with a sort of aerodynamic spoiler. As the weapon accelerated under the thrust of its cordite charge to a given speed, the spoiler was to be forced open by the wind speed, interrupt the airflow and divert the rocket at right angles before snapping off under pressure.

It seemed worth a try, although it sounded somewhat haphazard; and so it proved. A demonstration was arranged and a distinguished audience of interested spectators gathered for the trials. A battery of rocket launchers was mounted to the flank of their observation stand and the first salvo was fired. Unfortunately owing to some miscalculation or misfortune (surely not with intent?) the rockets duly diverted; but through 180° not 90° as planned. They screamed back over the heads of the terrified spectators (for some of whom it was the first time they had really earned the Africa Stars they proudly displayed) and crashed into the sand behind them. There were no casualties, but the experiment was abandoned.

We continued assiduously with our established tactics and were kept pretty busy. Even at base life was not without incident. While at Mersa Matruh we had the pleasure of the company of a squadron of Royal Hellenic Air Force Spitfires (the enemy was by now trying very little in the way of counter-attack but sensible precautions had to be taken). In the spring of 1944, we had the privilege of a visit from one of the best known and bizarre figures to emerge from the Desert Campaign. His name was Jasper Maskelyne, well known before the war as a partner in the great team of theatrical magicians and illusionists, Maskelyne and Devant. His natural talents for deception had been put to excellent use and his neatest trick was the production of dummy aircraft in large numbers. Made of wood and fabric, they were startlingly lifelike from the air, defying both visual and photographic reconnaissance. Dressed up as a Colonel in the Camouflage Corps, or some such, he would arrive on an airfield with a few truckloads of materials and a band of enthusiastic specialists and, hey presto! in a matter of hours squadrons of bombers or fighters materialized where God and the Air Ministry had created none.

As a man he was vastly entertaining and a great raconteur and personally always a welcome arrival on a desert airfield. Professionally his visits tended to be less acceptable, since in the nature of things as soon as the enemy detected these instant reinforcements a rain of bombs tended to follow.

At this time the Allies were going to great lengths to try to confuse and deceive the enemy as to where our invasion of Europe, by now clearly pending, would be directed. The ' soft under-belly ' could by no means be ruled out of German calculations (and indeed as noted was at one time Winston Churchill's favoured solution). Naturally everything possible was being done to foster this illusion, and Colonel Maskelyne's Circus was kept hard at it, generating squadrons of cardboard bombers up and down the coast of North Africa for the enemy to detect and draw false conclusions from. At Mersa Matruh we were honoured with the appearance of two squadrons of lifelike Liberator heavy bombers.

Now enemy activity against us at this stage was confined as a rule to a weekly visitation from a special reconnaissance Ju86P which came over at very high level indeed and photographed our airfields; the old Spitfires dutifully chased it but its height and speed were usually beyond them. With Teutonic thoroughness it visited us regularly on Thursdays (or Fridays if the weather prevented the Thursday trip). Our massive Liberators sat there waiting to be photographed and strict instructions were given to the defences to make sure that the photography was not prevented. Thursday came, and Friday; but no reconnaissance. We were a little disturbed but rationalized that the weather was probably bad at the Greek bases; all would be well next week. But next week came and went still without sight or sound of our regular customer; and now there was growing cause for concern, for sand, sun and wind soon undid Jasper's work, which was not designed to last and only retained its realistic appearance from the air for quite a short period.

It was with some relief that a day or two later we received a report from the Air Defence Centre of an incoming track, fast, very high and headed straight for us. All would soon be well and the deceptive photographs duly taken. Alas! for the best laid plans etc. In a moment of mental aberration, carried away by the lust for battle, or merely through lack of linguistic communication, one of our gallant Greek allies managed to haul his ageing Spitfire well above its normal ceiling and to shoot down the intruder. Amid yells of Hellenic enthusiasm and bellows of British fury the Junkers crashed into the sea in flames a mile or so from the airfield.

By what must have been a unique statistic, this one sortie achieved for the pilot at the same time a Greek DFC and a British court martial.

I was myself coming to the end of another operational tour, and took some much needed leave. A fellow officer and I decided that Palestine would make a nice break from the Western Desert, especially as he had a cousin living in Jerusalem who kindly offered us accommodation. The cousin turned out to be an amusing rugged character, who held some high police appointment which kept him pretty busy. We were thus left largely to our own devices and made the most of the archaeology, the scenery and also the flesh-pots of Jerusalem. Starting one evening's entertainment in the bar of the King David Hotel, still intact at the time, I was hailed by an old acquaintance. We exchanged drinks and news. He asked where I was staying and, when I identified my host, stared at me in astonishment: ' My God, you're either bloody brave or bloody stupid. Don't you get shot at enough on your squadron? '.

' What d'you mean? '

' Jimmy W your host. Don't you know he's the current Number One on the Stern Gang's list? They've announced publicly they'll get him in a month—you too, I expect, if you stay there much longer.'

We did not. Somewhat cravenly and ungratefully, we cleared off and spent the rest of our leave in Beirut where at least only our moral welfare was at risk. We learned later that the Stern Gang successfully fulfilled their threat.

On return, I was posted once more to Glorious Gambut where after a short spell as Wing Commander Operations, I was given the command of No 603 (City of Edinburgh) Auxiliary Air Force Squadron. The operational job and the aircraft were the same as on my previous tour.

I have written earlier of the merits of the auxiliaries. By now of course, after nearly five years of war, none of the original aircrew remained on the squadron, but a large proportion of the groundcrew were prewar squadron members, some of them even founder members of the squadron with nearly twenty years unbroken service. The value of the continuing cohesive spirit of these tough, loyal Edinburgh men was immeasurable. It was their squadron. They had seen it through some very rough times in the Battle of Britain and in Malta; and they were quite happy to go on doing so just as long as they were needed.

The Senior Squadron Member was a splendid old man named Warrant Officer Prentice, who was the lynch-pin of the whole organization and a mine of both history and legend. He argued firmly that his age was 'juist about 50' but as his son was also an NCO on the squadron, this was a little difficult to credit (particularly as rumour had it that his grandson was also about to join us). One sad day the blow fell. Authority in Cairo ruled that, now the critical pressures had eased, the Western Desert was no place for old men to serve and that all those over 50 years of age should be posted home. We wriggled and evaded and procrastinated, but the end was inevitable. Mr Prentice was to go home to Edinburgh.

We gave him a full ceremonial farewell parade, although the uniforms were not quite of Horse Guards standard. Gambut offered few shopping facilities, so instead of a presentation piece, we had a whip-round to which every man on the squadron contributed. After months in the Desert, most pockets were pretty well lined and I had great pleasure in presenting the old man with a cheque for well over £100; which he accepted with dignity and apparently just as great pleasure.

Three months later the Squadron was once again back in the United Kingdom and everyone was delighted when Warrant Officer Prentice immediately rejoined us. I had the tact not to ask about the cheque, and Mr Prentice had the good taste not to refer to it either.

Our war in the Aegean was reaching its end. There were still some targets to be attacked, the ships often by now attempting not to reinforce or resupply the garrisons but to evacuate them. Our task was to prevent them reaching the mainland and strengthening the occupying forces that still held it in an iron grip. The enemy's defences were weaker and perhaps also his spirit, for which he could scarcely be blamed. There were problems with isolated island garrisons, cut off and with no offensive capability but still reasonably armed and entrenched; they would have taken a lot of dislodging had they decided to fight it out. To discourage them from doing so we attacked their barracks and gun positions with rocket and cannon; but this was not always easy since the barracks were often in the centre of towns and villages and we wanted to avoid killing our Greek friends, whose hardships and deprivations were already extreme.

This situation provided for me one of the classic signals of all time (I still preserve it). The target of the mission was a small German force in the island town of Kalymnos. The executive signal from Higher Authority to me as leader read, ' Pilots will not, repeat not, open fire but will fly in such a manner as to leave no doubt in the minds of the enemy that his fate is sealed '.

After some debate and tooth sucking, we finally interpreted this oracle by flying over the town at low level upside down. Oddly enough, it did the trick.

In early October 1944, I was instructed to take three aircraft to the neighbouring airfield of El Adem. There we were to join Anthony Eden, the

Foreign Secretary, and provide fighter escort for his flight into newly liberated Athens. I had not had the privilege of meeting this distinguished man previously, but talking to him before lunch, found him a most interesting and interested companion. I informed him about the arrangements for his escort and he enquired where my other officers were. I told him they were lunching in the Transit Mess. He turned to the Station Commander on his other side: 'Please have them sent for immediately. If they are good enough to fly with me, they are certainly good enough to sit down at lunch with me '.

A few days later in Athens, in the midst of all the complications and problems of that difficult time, we chanced to meet again while sightseeing on the Acropolis. We admitted to being a bit blown having walked up from the town. He immediately arranged for transport to be put at our disposal. To my mind these little touches were the mark of a great man, and I stored them away carefully.

Our flight to Athens had been uneventful and our welcome was initially overwhelming. There were as always sour and bitter notes in the general rejoicing; private grudges and public shaming are the inevitable background to liberation. One unfortunate girl whose hair had received the ritual shave I recall especially, for no other reason than that in later years she became one of the most vociferous and highly publicized critics of the Papadopoulos regime. Her anti-Fascist enthusiasm was apparently not of very long standing—but then ladies are traditionally permitted to change their minds.

A happier encounter at a liberation party was with a particularly beautiful young woman. I was naturally in uniform and she asked me what I was flying; she expressed great interest when I mentioned Beaufighters and gradually the whole story came out.

She was the only daughter of a wealthy Greek tobacco tycoon. They had lived in a large handsome, old fashioned house near the centre of Athens. When the Germans invaded, the house was commandeered as a Mess for very senior German officials. Three or four of the latter took over the main living accommodation. The family were allowed to stay on as servants in the basement quarters. The father acted as steward/butler, the mother cooked; the daughter served as maid and waitress; and the son-in-law performed the manual chores below stairs, cleaning the boots and silver, stoking the boiler, emptying the garbage and so on. The incredible thing was that the Germans above stairs never noticed that the appearance and build of the son-in-law changed at intervals. He was in fact the British officer at the time passing through a staging post of the underground escape route opened up by the Resistance. From Athens each was in turn smuggled to Corinth and then to the Peloponnese for a rendezvous with a British submarine and final escape. In recent years the escapers had naturally usually been shot-down aircrew.

Learning that I had been flying Beaufighters in the area for more than a year, the daughter asked me: ' Do you by any chance know Snowy Peters?'

' Yes, indeed I do—of course he evaded successfully didn't he? I suppose he passed through here—why do you ask about him particularly?'

' Oh, nothing very important. D'you expect to see him again? '

' Yes, almost certainly I imagine.'

' Would you give him a message from me? You see, he had to stay with us quite a while, and—well—he took his position as son-in-law of the house quite seriously. Will you tell him he now has a fine son? '.

I was astonished. ' But surely you want to get in touch with him more than that? I can probably arrange for him to come over and see you.'

' No, no—everything's all right. You see, 1 happen to know he was married. We'll both be perfectly well looked after from now on—but I thought he'd like to know about his son. He's fair haired and looks just like Snowy—same thirst, too.'

End of story; and our time in Greece was to end abruptly too. There was really little justification for our staying on, and when ELAS, ELAM and various other noxious organizations began to shoot at their glorious liberators we decided that we had outstayed our welcome and returned to Gambut.

With the collapse of German resistance in Greece and the Aegean our job was completed and there was much speculation about our future, both as a unit and as individuals. I was much concerned, especially as other squadrons were being disbanded and their people dispersed in all directions. I need not have worried; the Royal Auxiliary Air Force ' Union ' was very powerful. The Lord Provost of Edinburgh, then the great and good Sir Willy Y. Darling, made forcible enquiries at high level about the whereabouts of and plans for ' his ' squadron. 603 Squadron retained its entity and very shortly afterwards was on a troopship steaming home through the now secure Mediterranean. This also saved my own bacon; I had already been warned that I was to be given a ground appointment at last, as CO of a rather dreary Egyptian support base called Idku. I was very grateful to Sir Willy.

On the voyage home, in the intervals of almost non-stop bridge games, I could look back with pleasure and perhaps with some satisfaction on my Middle East interlude. Our end of the war had been on a miniature scale compared to Overlord or Stalingrad; but, although it may have been a backwater, we had cleaned it up successfully. We had been given a specific job to do and we had done it. I had not only managed to survive once more but I had found an operational role which suited me and at which I had become reasonably proficient (I had been recommended for a DFC, had been mentioned in despatches, and become an acting Wing Commander). I had largely overcome my own apprehensions and acquired the ability to lead men in battle. And I think I had already absorbed the basic lesson of leadership, that those who are led are just as important as their leaders; that leadership is not just a matter of Chiefs and Indians, but of closely interdependent strata of responsibility; and that acknowledgment of and dependence on subordinates is perhaps the most important element of any successful military structure.

Ever since then I have, I hope, avoided the besetting sin of doing my colleagues' or subordinates' jobs for them. This may not derive from wise judgment or experience; it may be basically rooted in indolence. Whatever the cause, I have never, or only extremely rarely, had cause to doubt its rightness. Admittedly in the RAF one has been unusually blessed because the basic quality of the men, buttressed by the high standard of their training enables one to rely and depend. I have only one or two small scratches from broken reeds to show for several decades of applying this principle. It also works both ways, in that when a man, be he an engine fitter or a senior air staff officer, knows that he is relied on, he will do everything in his power to justify that reliance and his performance will improve accordingly.

I have been sorry to note that this principle, so self-evident to me, is not appreciated by many of my colleagues in the Armed Forces. There is still a great deal too much (to my mind) of peering over shoulders, of ham-handed and otiose supervision for supervision's sake. A man who does not trust his subordinates is really indicating that he does not trust himself—and probably justifiably. Years later I shocked a very senior associate by admitting complete ignorance of a matter about which he had gone to great lengths to acquaint himself. He thought I was wrong and casual in my approach; I thought he was wrong to interfere in or duplicate work that was being admirably done at a lower level. It is a matter of opinion.

One final element of my life belongs in this chapter. My love affair with the Aegean and its islands, where eventually I was to build a home, had flowed originally from the roots of a classical education and a bent for Hellenic archaeology; having now witnessed the beauty of two or three dozen Aegean dawns, I knew that I must return there under happier circumstances.

8   The Last Round

Our voyage home was swift and uneventful, since by then the U-boat threat had been largely mastered. I had still of course the responsibility of command but officers and men were in good heart and there were few problems. I say I still had the responsibility of command but some people apparently deemed otherwise. A while later when I became entitled, as I thought, to a seniority increment to my Wing Commander's pay it was not forthcoming. When I enquired about this, the Air Ministry replied shortly that during the actual voyage home 603 Squadron had officially ceased to exist, and had only recovered its identity on the date of our arrival in the UK. Consequently my acting rank of Wing Commander had suffered the same fate and was revived only from the same date. I suppose the author of the letter was proud of his war effort; he was by no means a unique example of his profession.

In the midst of much rumour and speculation about our eventual destination, we arrived at Liverpool by night and found a special train awaiting the squadron. Still in ignorance of where we were going, we spent the night travelling through the blacked-out country and anonymous railway stations, vainly trying to deduce our direction and whereabouts; Carlisle, Nottingham and Swindon were each in turn confidently recognised—which seemed improbable. Early in the morning we fetched up at what proved to be Norwich and found transport waiting to take us to our nearby base, Coltishall. I was personally quite happy about this, but many of the groundcrew were naturally disappointed to be so far from Edinburgh.

The programme was that all were to be given statutory disembarkation leave and then reunite to fly as a squadron on the Coltishall Wing. The adjutant and I spent a busy morning in the Headquarters on the necessary administrative chores but found in fact that the Station organization already had things well in hand. Nominal rolls had miraculously preceded us; railway warrants were awaiting details; leave-passes were ready. We were much impressed by the smooth running of the unit. Its commander was an old friend, Arthur Donaldson, one of the legendary Donaldson family of three brothers and a cousin whose operational war record was unique. It was good to feel that we were going to be well looked after and well led.

By lunchtime the needs of the men were all arranged, and Arthur and I adjourned to the Mess bar, where my aircrew officers were already obviously enjoying themselves—especially the company of some very attractive WAAF officers, something we had not encountered for a long while. One turned out to be an old Oxford friend and I showed my officers a good example of establishing good relations with the natives.

Over a couple of pints, Arthur and I sorted out a few more matters of detail (I was going off on leave with the others after lunch). He said, ' Oh, one small point, Chris. What are your squadron's identifying letters? We'll get them painted on your Spitfires so that you can start operating as soon as you get back '.

I choked on my beer. ' Say that again slowly, Sir.'

' Your squadron letters, man, for painting on your Spitfires.'

' That's what I thought you said, Sir. Now please look around carefully at my officers—does anything strike you as unusual about them? '

' No, I don't think so . . . There seems to be rather a lot of them . . . and, good God, half of them are wearing observer's wings! '

' That's right, Sir. We're a Beaufighter anti-shipping squadron.'

' Well, there's a thing. We, you may be surprised to know, are a Spitfire tactical wing—we spend most of our time now dive bombing V-2 sites.'

I did not go on leave that afternoon. Frenzied telephoning eventually disclosed that some mastermind at the Air Ministry had overlooked the fact that the Squadron had re-equipped to Beaufighters from Spitfires on leaving Malta in 1942. Of course, nearly all the auxiliary ground crew were well experienced on Spitfires. But, of the pilots only myself and another couple had ever flown one, and that non-operationally; and what about our 20-odd observers?

At this stage, I had an inspiration. I remembered that our old boss and mentor, Max Aitken, was now commanding the anti-shipping wing at Banff in Scotland (albeit equipped with Mosquitos). I reached once more for the telephone. Could he use 23 experienced anti-shipping crews? He certainly could, or at least most of them. The Banff Wing had four squadrons and had been experiencing the usual heavy losses; these, sadly but fortunately for me, included the CO of my old squadron No 143, a very gallant French officer called Meurice.

Max, who of course had unusual channels of communication and areas of influence, duly fixed the whole thing. All the 603 aircrew, with the exception of a few already nearly tour-expired, were posted to the Banff Wing after their disembarkation leave. The only unhappy aspect of an otherwise ideal solution, was that we were parted from our auxiliary ground-crew who stayed on at Coltishall to re-form the squadron with a new batch of pilots. They were used to this and took it in their stride; but I was sad once again to move out of the blessed world of the auxiliary air force with all its special ties and strengths.

I took over command of 143 Squadron and found a few familiar faces still there from 18 months back; with the rest of the 603 crews I did a quick conversion to the Mosquito without leaving Banff. It presented few problems and was of course a legendary aircraft. Its speed and manoeuvrability and consequent ability to look after itself were far better than those of the dear old Beaufighter, which however held the edge in its robust ability to absorb anti-aircraft fire. Our Mosquitos were the Mark VI, specially tuned for low level operations, and of course slowed to some extent by their loads of rockets and the rails for them fitted under the wings, and by the carriage of underslung long-range tanks. Nevertheless we were very happy with them, and could not wait to try them out in action.

The operational role was not unlike that we had already practised in the Aegean, only this time the shipping we were trying to interdict was that operating along the Norwegian coast; and the characteristics of the latter added considerably to our difficulties. The hundreds of fjords and leads that lace that coast gave innumerable hiding places for shipping, which indeed for much of its passage could operate inside the island chain; and when we did find the targets the steepness of the mountain sides falling to the water made the actual attack a most difficult and hazardous performance. The main anchorages were very well protected and one had on occasion the novel and unpleasant experience of being fired on from above by anti-aircraft guns emplaced on steep hillsides. Illogically this made us feel much more vulnerable in our little perspex greenhouses—illogically, because we had no more protection from below than a thin skin of wood and our parachute packs (although we did have back-armour). One evening on returning from an attack, I had my attention drawn by my grinning groundcrew to a cannon shell which had penetrated my parachute and whose nose had finished in a position where a couple of inches further penetration would have severely handicapped my enjoyment of life in the future. What made it worse was that when extracted it proved to be one of our own—a ricochet I have always imagined (and hoped). On examination it did not prove to have my name on it.

We had four Mosquito squadrons on the Wing and on the neighbouring airfield of Dallachy four Beaufighter squadrons. Nearby at Peterhead was the Mustang fighter wing that sometimes gave us fighter escort. Their pilots, who included Bob Weighhill, later England's captain on the Rugger field, were brave men, because at least we had a second engine on which to come home in case of battle damage or mechanical failure. They had only one, and must have listened very intently to its beat as they crossed the 400 miles of icy North Sea that lay between us and our target area; the Mustang, like other low wing monoplane fighters, was not a good aircraft to ditch. One of the Mosquito squadrons was officially a unit of the Norwegian Air Force and very largely Norwegian manned. Like the Czechs, Poles and other Europeans they had escaped from their countries after the Germans invaded; in many cases had no news of their families, or knew that they had been killed; and in consequence were very determined and vengeful fighters. Their local knowledge was of great value not only geographically but also from the point of view of selection of targets and even of identification of collaborators. For example, they were able to tell us that the Norwegian coastguard had refused to operate certain lighthouses critical to the passage of German convoys. The lights were now either manned by Germans or by Quisling supporters and therefore were open to attack on an opportunity basis. Attacks on the lanterns with cannonfire were rather fun—something like cutting off the top of one's breakfast egg in happier times.

Targets were not only plentiful but important. With the advance of the Allied armies and with the attacks of Bomber Command on Germany itself, the iron ore supplies of Scandinavia were becoming increasingly important if the enemy munitions and war material factories were to be kept going. They took considerable risks in trying to run their convoys; and once again losses were high on both sides. Again, as in the Aegean, our own were largely to anti-aircraft fire; fighter interceptions were haphazard as we were usually able to evade the radar cover. When we were intercepted, it was unpleasant, as a rocket-racked Mosquito was no match for a Focke Wulf 190. Our only real tactic was to depend on the Mustangs for cover if they were with us; otherwise to run for it. One day I was leading the wing back under very poor visibility conditions. Unaware of any particular threat, I was flying only at fast cruising speed. All of a sudden to my surprise, my 30 or so loyal comrades sprinted past me, and in a few seconds I had fallen from first place to last. I had unknowingly sustained radio failure (we kept radio silence except in the attack or in emergency). Our rear section had reported enemy fighters closing from behind. Everyone had opened to full throttle, except the temporarily deaf leader. I guessed what was afoot and took immediate steps to resume my rightful position up front. Fortunately in the event they missed us in the fog and low cloud.

Other encounters were less happy. We tended naturally to break up during an actual attack and the escape from the target area too often produced a straggle. Whereas, as always, the leaders tended to bear the brunt of the flak, it was the tailenders who paid for it if we were intercepted. At Banff I had managed to keep the same second-in-command who had been with me in the Desert. He was a very remarkable character by the name of Tommy Deck. Short, thick set, red haired and noisy he had a wonderful fighting record. Universally admired and liked, he was quite literally fearless. This is an overused and misused word but I genuinely believe that he never felt fear. Indeed, a sortie which produced no opposition was a relief to the rest of us, but a dead bore to Tommy. Very early one morning we managed to sneak into Andalsnes harbour and attack an anchored convoy before we were detected. For once we got away practically scot-free because we had caught the anti-aircraft defences napping. This was not good enough for Tommy. He proceeded to fly round and round the harbour shooting up the anti-aircraft crews to encourage them to do better next time.

Another time he was hit in his starboard engine during the attack and forced to feather one propeller. As we left the target area we heard with concern radio calls indicating that our rear sections, which Tommy was leading, had been jumped by Focke-Wulfs and were having a bad time. We were too far away to be able to get back to help out in time but Tommy was not; he turned back on his one engine and joined in the scrap. He got away with it—and apparently enjoyed it enormously. I suspect he would have been quite happy to fight Mohammed Ali with one hand tied behind his back.

As previously in Cornwall, life for No 143 and the other squadrons was pretty good when off duty. Personally in fact I was not overemployed on operational flying. It took some time to re-muster, repair and re-service the wing after a mass strike and targets for the wing were not always available or detected; so we very rarely attacked in strength more than two or three times a week, although of course there were individual reconnaissances to be flown to find our targets. There were three or four regular leaders for the Wing, so one only led at most once a week, which probably meant not more than half a dozen operational flights a month, although of course there was training to be done and a lot of organization and personnel work to deal with as a Commanding Officer. When not so employed, one was handsomely entertained by the local people, particularly Nina, Countess of Seafield, who more or less ran her neighbouring castle as an extension to the Officers' Mess.

Rationing did not really bite in Northern Scotland and we ate and drank well, and usually seemed to be able to scrounge some petrol for recreational purposes. These included a memorable organized visit to the neighbouring Grant's distillery. Ever the natural leader, Max decided to conduct this operation in person with suitable support. All went well until at the end of the programme, already nicely primed with the odd sampling on our tour, we gathered for a farewell drink at the Directors' Table. Before each of us was a half tumbler of a dark liquid, which proved to be a whisky of over 50 years of age and of quite incredible smoothness and strength. Our conductor assured us that it would not be sacrilege to dilute it, which we proceeded to do from the apparent decanters of water before us. Too late we realized that they too contained an equally ancient and powerful whisky, but from white wood casks rather than oak, and therefore colourless. We found out later that this was a traditional jest and the local villagers, forewarned, gathered to get a lot of free and innocent enjoyment from watching the distinguished guests attempting to re-enter their motor cars.

There was of course in those remote parts also the problem of sex. Instincts were natural and perhaps more pressing than usual because of the lurking uncertainty of survival. One of my officers was unfortunately detected by a WAAF NCO on his off-duty morning, cosily bedded with his batwoman. We duly lined up in front of the Group Captain; the officer concerned charged with conduct unbecoming or some such; myself as his CO; the young lady involved (corpus delicti?); her Squadron Officer; and the WAAF NCO who was the chief witness.

Max looked at the papers. 'Ah, yes', he said, after a while. 'Now who's going to tell me about this?'

'I will, Sir', said the Squadron Officer stoutly. 'It is a straightforward but most unfortunate case. Sergeant Walkeley, making her routine morning rounds, discovered this officer and this WAAF in a most compromising position which left no doubt in her mind as to their relationship and—er—their activities.'

Max looked up. 'Yes?' he asked.

The Squadron Officer blushed. 'Well, Sir, if you insist on my being more explicit, Sir, they were in bed together, and—er—unclothed.'

'Yes?' repeated Max.

The Squadron Officer was by now not only embarrassed but also angry.

' Sir, you force me into a very awkward position. If you compel me to be entirely frank, Sir, Sergeant Walkeley interrupted this officer actually making love to this girl, one of my WAAF's.'

' Oh, yes ', said Max mildly, ' but after all that is what they're here for, isn't it? '

Up to a point I suppose it was. We were young, tough, reasonably virile, highly strung and emotional and very isolated. When we were off duty we demanded wine, women and song. It would have been illogical perhaps to provide only two out of three. In any case, whatever the moralities (or immoralities) of the case, the girls and women concerned performed their Service duties admirably. The original idea of the women's armed forces had been to release men for more arduous or hazardous tasks; in the event it often proved that the women did their jobs better than the men they replaced. Whatever else can be said for or against war, it certainly provides a great boost for women's lib. The female factory and farm workers of World War I could not be treated as inferior citizens again when peace came; much less the female ferry pilots, air mechanics, secret agents and other less glamorous participants in World War II. So far they have stopped short, at least in the armed forces of the West, of combat status. Who knows how long before we take this next step, following the example of the Communist comrades?

One of my less usual claims to fame until the Spring of 1945 was that I had never dropped a bomb in anger, in spite of being on flying duties continuously since 1939; few could make the same claim since even the great fighter aces like the Donaldsons and Johnny Johnson mostly played their part in fighter-bomber attacks after the battle of air superiority was won. In February 1945 1 dropped my first and last bombs; they were four in number and they were unfused. Before the armourer's union rush to defend themselves, let me hastily add that they were intentionally unfused.

What happened was this. A lone reconnaissance aircraft from the Wing discovered quite unexpectedly, a large group of enemy vessels in the harbour of Egesund. It was too late in the day to assemble and mount a major strike and our aircraft were in any case still being recovered and repaired from the last one. This meant that the enemy ships, already showing signs of getting up steam, would have that evening and the long Northern night in which to be marshalled into convoy and steamed perhaps a hundred miles in either direction; or perhaps dispersed in several directions. They would take a lot of finding again in the innumerable fjords and waterways of the Norwegian coast.

We racked our brains for a solution when the reconnaissance report arrived; and someone finally came up with a brainwave. Shortly afterwards I took off and flew at maximum speed to Egesund just managing to arrive in daylight. I flew directly across the mouth of the harbour and dropped a stick of 250-pounders. They splashed harmlessly into the water and sank without further explosion. The Germans drew the hoped-for conclusion. The infernal English had mined the entrance; there could be no thought of leaving until the mines were swept. A nuisance and an unfortunate delay.

Next morning a highly successful attack was launched against the still-anchored ships. My reputation as Bomber Norris was made for ever.

Our main role was to seek and sink the enemy's ships but inevitably we also ran into his aircraft. One of my crews indeed met one of the earliest German jets, an Arado, on reconnaissance over the North Sea. The jet was of course very much faster but, well handled, the Mosquito was more manoeuvrable. My pilot had a strenuous few minutes of it before the Arado broke off the contest and disappeared; his nerves received a further shock when the de-briefing intelligence officer kindly told him that the Arado had been unarmed.

A more bloody encounter happened shortly afterwards. I had led a large force of Mosquitos over to the southern coast of Norway with a top cover of our faithful Mustangs. Unhappily when we entered the target area, it proved to be unexpectedly blanketed in mist and heavy rain and we found no targets. After searching about for some while, I gave the frustrated wing the order to turn for home, for which we set course with all our rockets and cannon undischarged. After about an hour, when we were well out of reach of enemy interception, the leader of the Mustangs, a good friend of mine named Pete Wykeham (not the future Air Marshal, then still Wykeham-Barnes) called me up. He sought permission to press on ahead as they had a big party laid on in the Peterhead Mess that night; the Mustang had a higher transit speed than our loaded Mosquitos. I readily agreed and the fighters accelerated away homewards.

We were still in bad weather, with rain and a cloud base of under 600ft and poor visibility. Suddenly we sighted quite a large force of aircraft approaching on a more or less reciprocal course. Seconds later we were able to identify them. They were a mixed bunch of Ju88 and Heinkel aircraft, returning from an equally abortive anti-shipping mission off the Scottish coast and heavily laden with bombs and torpedoes. An absolute massacre developed. We outnumbered them by more than two to one and our aircraft performance was far superior. Mosquitos were pushing and shoving like housewives in a bread queue to get at their unfortunate targets, which were plunging into the sea in all directions. When we finally got home and debriefed, we were to everybody's satisfaction credited with destroying 11 out of 18; and we reckoned a lot more were damaged before they staggered up into the cloud cover.

There was naturally great rejoicing at Banff and much publicity: coincidentally my DSO came through at about the same time which called for some extra drinks. We gathered there was also much chuckling and gloating at Coastal Command HQ where our C-in-C, Sholto Douglas, enjoyed himself ringing up the C-in-C of Fighter Command and offering fighter escort to his Mustangs when and if required. The latter dignitary naturally fell upon the unfortunate Peter Wykeham like a ton of bricks, and the whole affair was quite a nine-days' wonder. Indeed, as it turned out, not so much nine days as twenty-four years, as I will explain.

In 1969 as an Air Marshal I was commanding Royal Air Force, Germany, and also NATO's Second Allied Tactical Air Force, made up of ourselves,

the Dutch, the Belgians and half the Luftwaffe. Its operations were controlled from a Joint Operations Centre near Maastricht in Holland. This
was internationally staffed; the CO was a Belgian; the second in Command,
Colonel Hans Geisemann, a very gallant Luftwaffe pilot and one of their
great anti-shipping aces in the Mediterranean, three times shot down over
Malta convoys; the Senior British Officer was Wing Commander Bob
Golightly, who had been with me at Banff and participated in the action just
described.

He and Geisemann became good friends, and over a beer one evening
were reminiscing, as pilots always will, about the war, Geisemann observed:
' You know, Bob, one of the troubles with wars is that after a while one
forgets all the horrors and fears and remembers only the good things, the
comradeship, the decorations, the successes—the good days. I suppose it's
human nature, but, my God, we all had our bad days too. D'you know,
Bob, I once lost an entire wing—18 out of 18—in one action; two actually
got back to base but they were badly shot up and crashed trying to land.'

' That must have been very dreadful for you, Hans ', said Golightly,
' What were the circumstances? '

' Oh, it was right towards the end of the war. I was commanding a wing
of clapped out Junkers and Heinkels with scarcely trained crews in Norway.
I was told to send them out on 15 April, and . . .'

' Hold it a minute, Hans ', said Golightly. He went to his office, sorted
out his well-illustrated wartime logbook and brought it back. ' D'you mean
that time? '

And he did; we had destroyed the lot. It was one of the rare instances of
underclaiming in a war where both sides habitually exaggerated their successes
and played down their losses, sometimes in error, sometimes dishonestly,
often for propaganda purposes.

Sholto Douglas had previously been my C-in-C in the Middle East.
Although very different in character and personality he and Max shared
one attribute. They demanded success and were quite intolerant of failure.
This is doubtless a basic asset in a Commander; but it is overdone if the
intolerance extends alike to inevitable and the inexcusable failure, and fails
to differentiate between them. I will illustrate what I mean.

In late March 1945 a good friend of mine was leading the Wing on what
was potentially a dramatic mission. We had recently been re-equipped
with 2×100-gallon drop-tanks as an optional replacement for our previous
50-gallon ones. This gave us greatly increased range and enabled us for the
first time to penetrate over Denmark into the Skaggerak and Kattegat. The
Germans knew very well what our maximum range had been until then;
and beyond it they scarcely bothered to provide escort, certainly anti-aircraft
escort, for their shipping. We had managed to keep our new penetrative
capability secret from them and the Wing's first ultra-long-range outing
promised a rich harvest.

The promise was unfulfilled. More than 30 Mosquitos swept in over
Denmark and out over the sea to the East; but once again the weather
turned against them and for half an hour they searched in bad visibility with

64

no sign of a target. At the end of their endurance they found some, but pretty small fry, eight landing craft making their way North unloaded. The frustrated pilots swept down on them and expended their rockets and cannon-shells in sinking them all; but it was a disappointing bag.

Scattered and out of ammunition the Wing swung away to start on their long flight home. As they did so the flank aircraft spotted a 14,000-ton German troopship, steaming South from Norway to Kiel with a minimal escort and packed with reinforcements for the Eastern Front. There was nothing they could do to her except pepper her with the last few cannon shells left to them and take photographs.

It was a terrible let down and a great disappointment; but it was nobody's fault, just bad luck. Nevertheless Max, and indeed Sholto, did not forgive what they interpreted as failure.

Our new fuel tanks soon proved their worth, however (although one of mine nearly killed me when, on being jettisoned from low level, it bounced up and almost severed my tail plane), and with an increase in enemy shipping traffic, targets multiplied. At the time one of the options under consideration by the Germans was a strongly reinforced Fortress Norway, where they might hold out in the mountains and bargain with the Allies. Apart from that, there were a lot of ships escaping northwards as the Russians advanced through Danzig and the Baltic ports. One day, the Wing found four un-completed, undefended submaries escaping north on the surface. It was butchery but a butchery of the butchers. In sinking the lot we should have been untouched, but ironically we lost one aircraft.

We had been accompanied, as we often were, by a Mosquito of the RAF Film Unit. These aircraft were flown by specialist crews of great courage; they took all the risks of the operational crews but were themselves armed only with their cameras. As the last of the U-boats was driven down, the film pilot swooped very low to record its death throes. It blew up literally in his face (it may have been carrying mines) and no trace of him or his aircraft was ever found.

The Germans were obviously staggering more and more on their last legs, and all the Allied Forces mustered their strength for the final knock-out punch. On 3 May Sholto Douglas decided that all his shipping strike wings from Norfolk to North Scotland should carry out a last crushing co-ordinated strike. The weather was good over Britain and nearly every Wing had a successful day. The Banff Wing alone achieved nothing; crossing Denmark eastwards they ran into very heavy thunderstorms and turbulence, broke up and returned in small groups with their tails between their legs; but at least it cost no aircraft or men.

Sholto did not take kindly to this and nor did Max. The former rang up the latter to discuss the matter and, while expressing some sympathy, added some acid comment about it being a disappointing way to end the war in which the Wing had done so well. Max's mind was made up. The Wing would strike again the next day; and it was my turn to lead. It was an unusual decision, because as I have explained we rarely operated en masse on consecutive days, because of the need for post-strike reconnaissance to locate fresh targets and the time and effort needed to reassemble and reservice a force of over 40 aircraft.

We were briefed early. Our objective was to be, as so often, shipping targets of opportunity in the Skaggerak and Kattegat. An unpleasant item of intelligence included in the briefing was that Aalborg airfield in Northern Denmark and not far from our transit track was shown by photographic reconnaissance to be occupied by several hundred German fighters (we did not learn until after the war was over that they had no fuel—such knowledge might have saved me a few grey hairs). We took off. The storms had cleared and the weather and visibility were excellent. We crossed over Denmark, fired at but unscathed, and came out over the sea North of Kiel.

Immediately in front of us, about 10 miles away, was a line of four Narvik class Destroyers, some of the newest and most heavily armed types in the German navy, and particularly bristling with anti-aircraft guns. I have talked before of the difference between moral and physical courage. Here was a classic example. The war was in its last hours as it proved. If I went into attack, I would be lucky only to lose a quarter or so of my aircraft and crews, almost certainly including myself; I would destroy at least 20 lives for a cause already won. Had I refused to attack on those grounds, in the circumstances described I would have faced inevitable court-martial for cowardice in the face of the enemy. It was a nice choice.

For some few, but seemingly endless seconds, we swept on towards the destroyers. Then my navigator, the faithful, imperturbable, invaluable Paddy Tuhill gave me a sharp nudge in the ribs.

' Look, Sir, down there. Three o'clock, about 12 miles.'

There, God save us, was an alternative target; two large merchant ships, comparatively lightly escorted by a frigate and two small anti-aircraft escorts. With a sigh of relief I swung the whole formation to starboard, marshalled them and led into the attack. We left all five ships blazing and sinking, and returned home thankfully; almost as we landed the war officially ended.

It was an interesting fact that, although every one of 40 or more crews behind me must have seen the four Narvik destroyers, not one reported them at de-briefing. Discretion is undoubtedly the better part of valour—if you are given a choice. My personal relief and elation were destroyed when I learnt that, although we had only lost one crew, the pilot Ian Thorburn was one of my oldest and dearest friends. He crashed attempting to force land on one engine in Sweden; he must have died literally in the last minutes of the war. It was a difficult thing to explain to his parents, who accepted it with the utmost gallantry and understanding.

For us all, the war was over. It had been a long one and we were very tired—I suppose I was one of the few survivors who had served on flying duties without a break from the first day to the last. We looked back with relief, sadness and some pride. We looked forward with doubt and apprehension.

9   Reprise

While a war is raging, few of those engaged in it have the time or the breadth of vision to look forward beyond their immediate sphere of activity.   High commanders presumably make jottings for history; but lesser mortals are too busy to learn any lessons but the empirical ones of tactics and survival. Only afterwards can one look back and try to draw some conclusions; and even then for most of us experience had been so narrowly and intensely focused that it was not easy to find answers to the broader questions.

Had it all been necessary?   I concluded then and believe now that it was. By 1939 at least, war had become the only means left to us to try to put the world to rights, or at least stop it going further wrong.   Earlier there may have been and probably were other methods and channels open to us; but we had missed our opportunities, and our own failures and the ambitions of the totalitarian dictators eventually made war as inevitable as Nemesis. The only alternative would have been to go quietly, to have bowed our own heads to the same totalitarianism.   Only the tiniest minority can ever have considered this as a real option.   So it was necessary.

Once necessary, had it been well conducted?   In parts, perhaps, but it was a very curate's egg affair.   It has become a customary ritual to blame all the setbacks and failures by either side in a war on the generals, the admirals and the air marshals.   It is, to me at least, an unattractive spectacle to observe the jackals of literature gleefully descending upon their prey (who, incidentally, while they are still serving are statutorily forbidden to defend themselves in print); but it seems to be a lucrative occupation; and, as ' muck makes brass ', so apparently in this field brass makes muck.   A dagger steeped in blood, preferably that of a friend, seems to pay well.

Let us not overlook however a few points in riposte.   Generals do not appoint themselves; they are appointed ultimately by politicians, who share in the glory of their successes but discreetly melt into the shadows when they fail.   Generals do not make national policy.   They fight when and where they are ordered and with the men and materials they are given; if the time or place is wrong and if the resources are inadequate, as in our national case they always are, at least initially, they have to do the best they can.   Often it is not a very good best—but who chose the time and the place and allotted the resources?   On occasion the politicians and the statesmen do not stop there, and actually interfere in the campaigns once launched.   Hitler was the worst offender in this field.   The victors of the Battle of Britain and of Stalingrad owe much to him; and his insistence on misusing the invention of the jet-engine saved us a lot of lives.   Nor was Churchill innocent of this connection, although at least his Generals could oppose him without fear of execution.

Let us not forget either that the demands made upon military men and military minds are often made by those who deny the need for military preparation in peace and affect to despise those who follow the profession of arms. All right—so the regular Services are supposed to consist of Colonel Blimp, Admiral Brassbound and Flying Officer Kite. But those who so misrepresent them as subhuman are the first to ask them to behave as superhumans when war comes. The Generals who were driven back across France and out through Dunkirk, and the Air Marshals who were expected to give them cover with the Lysander, the Fairey Battle and the biplane Gladiator were the same men, or the immediate successors of the men, who for nearly 20 years were starved of equipment and resources by the political ostriches of successive governments who imposed the notorious Ten Year Rule (all military budgets must be based on and limited by the assumption that there will be no war for ten years).

Perhaps a parable would illustrate: Once upon a time there was a rich man of great possessions who lived in a lordly mansion. But he, like so many rich men, was also a mean and miserly man. So, to protect his possessions and his demesne, he provided only a few guard dogs. These he fed inadequately so that, although of good breeding and spirit, they became undernourished and feeble. Furthermore on feast days and holidays, he and his lickspittle cronies would make mock of the dogs, calling them slow witted curs and forcing them to perform petty tricks to entertain the company. On a day, a great band of robbers burst in upon that demesne, consuming and devouring all the substance therein. The unhappy dogs fought gallantly but were too few and too weak to withstand. Then cried that rich man, ' Fools, cowards, poltroons! Did I not say that you could not be relied on? Was I not right to decry your strength and despise your breeding? Did I not . . .? ' At that moment a passing robber obligingly cut off his head and he was no more heard. O, si sic omnes.

A best selling book on World War I generals was entitled *The Donkeys;* perhaps its sequel covering World War II could be called ' The Scapegoats '. And for World War III . . .?

Let us be sure of one thing. If future governments adopt the now generally accepted policy of stripping the country's defences in time of peace (' Fire insurance, my dear chap? Why should I bother with fire insurance? Damned expensive, if you ask me, and we haven't had a fire for over 30 years. What? Yes, I know my neighbour's a pyromaniac but he s a good fellow at heart and has promised to behave better in future '), the results are horrifyingly and precisely predictable. And there will be no Dunkirk next time. Our potential enemies are not the same as last time, but they can read military history as well as the next man. At least the Generals will not be pilloried and criticized when it is all over, for the simple reason that the critics themselves will have been fused or fissioned or will be muzzled.

Englishmen traditionally celebrate a victory with a sporting word about their defeated adversary. Belsen, Dachau and a hundred others like them may make this inappropriate to the minds of most of us. But I suggest that no comments, however trivial, on World War II can fail to take note of the remarkable military achievements of the Third Reich. ' Come the whole world in arms and we will shock them '. Eventually nearly the whole world did come at them. They certainly shocked us and they came very close to beating us. Historians will make much of this remarkable achievement.

It is not easy to write publicly of one's personal part in war, since self-analysis is only of much interest to self. I could perhaps best sum it all up by saying that I survived, which was much against the odds; that I found myself capable of doing and enduring things which I had thought beyond my capability; that I learned quite a lot about leadership, both while leading and being led; that I found confidence, happiness and pride in the company of my fellow-men; that I made many friends, and unfortunately lost most of them. I became a realist, perhaps even a cynic. For the time being I had learnt to sift genuine values, real priorities and true men from the imitation.

Yet, ridiculous and perhaps deplorable though it may sound, some of it, as Hans Geisemann said, was very good fun. War for air forces is, and was always, an odd mixture. The actual combat is statistically more dangerous than for any other arm; but the intervals between combat can be spent in much greater comfort. ' Eat, drink and make merry for tomorrow we die ' is widely regarded as a pretentious and melodramatic cliche, but for aircrew it contains a lot of truth. The expectation of death, fully justified as it was, concentrates the mind wonderfully, to paraphrase Dr Johnson; and for two reasons one's horizon foreshortens remarkably. One is because tomorrow's prospects do not bear thinking about except by the very brave or the fatalistic; the second because the next day probably does not exist. So we ate, as far as rationing permitted. We drank with a regular, rather desperate excess which ruined many a digestion, including my own. And we made Merry (or indeed any other girl who happened to be available at the time). Unlike many of my contemporaries I avoided the entanglement of a war time marriage, perhaps more by good luck than by good management; and I think I may be grateful for it, because one's judgment at the time was clearly distorted and clouded with other issues.

So there were pros as well as cons, swings compensating for roundabouts. There is perhaps a danger here for the future. Man is a combative creature, born with aggressive instincts and a basic acquisitiveness. It is in his nature to envy other people and to desire their possessions. His animal instincts encourage him to try to take those possessions by force. If the process of doing so involves fighting, so be it. A lot of human beings follow their animal forbears in enjoying fighting per se as well as the rewards that derive from it. As long as wars can be enjoyable to any extent, and as long as we continue to breed generations of aggressive young people who can find both an outlet for that aggression and some personal enjoyment in its conduct, we shall always be threatened by war. Only when nuclear or biochemical weapons make war intolerably unpleasant for everyone actually or potentially engaged, shall we be free of this real risk to peace.

However, for myself the fear, the discomfort and the element of enjoyment were things of the past. I suppose I emerged as the traditional sadder and wiser man. What use was I going to make of all this sadness and wisdom?

10   Peace, Imperfect Peace

The first major peacetime decision that I made was to accept the permanent commission in the Royal Air Force that I had been recently offered. This meant discarding any idea of returning to the legal profession, and may be considered a waste of the time and money that had been put into my training for the Bar. There were several factors that tipped the balance, principally that my mind had been diverted into totally different channels for nearly six years. To divert it back again would have been much easier said than done because the whole routine of training had been interrupted. Like so many others, between the ages of eight (or indeed of five in my own case, because of my father's untimely death), and twenty-two, my way of life had consisted largely of attending boarding schools, receiving instruction, reading books and passing examinations; for which I personally developed a considerable knack. But it was a knack, and I had probably lost it. Without any false modesty, I reckoned that the Bar examinations which had been a few weeks away from me in 1939 were now at least a year, perhaps two, away. I had no money for sustenance for such a period and frankly little enthusiasm for the intellectual slog it would have involved.

I turned my back on the Bar (the first time I had done so for a long while, I might add). There was an interesting sequel in later years. In about 1952, by then married and impoverished as most officers were in that period, I received a courteous communication from the Treasurer of the Middle Temple which read much as follows:

> Dear Wing Commander,
>   Although our records show that in 1938 you received a Harmsworth Scholarship to the value of £200 pa for a period of three years, we note from our records that you have not yet been called. Would you please let me know your plans in this direction; or, if it would be more convenient, let me have your cheque for £600.
>   Yours etc

At that time any cheque of mine for £600, £60 or indeed probably £16 would have bounced, so I replied in some trepidation explaining the situation and laying the blame, where it justly rested, on Hitler. I was given most kindly and understanding treatment and a gentlemen's agreement was finally reached whereby in my Will the £600 would eventually be returned to the Inn for the use of a future Harmsworth Scholar. However, in view of the devaluation of the pound in the interval, I feel I perhaps should now make it £6,000. Let us hope that the sales of this book will make that possible.

The second factor in my decision was that I had enjoyed and was enjoying life in the Air Force. I thought that there was every chance of my continuing to enjoy it; and on the whole I did. Consequently, although it would not be true to say that I have never regretted the decision, the occasions on which I have done so have not been many or of long duration.

The immediate postwar weeks were a difficult time at Banff, as elsewhere. Max Aitken soon returned to his wide responsibilities in civilian life (although he offered generous hospitality in his luxurious flat to officers of the Wing who made their way to London for a little dissipation). He was replaced by an ageing officer who lacked operational background and therefore the essential understanding of operational aircrew. A difficult task for anyone thus became almost impossible for him—there were some awkward moments when one had to stand between authority and one's offending flock, protecting the latter while trying not to undermine the former.

At about this time, the Air Ministry decided, for reasons undisclosed at my level at least, but probably because there were still a lot of German aircraft sitting about in the area, to send a wing of RAF Spitfires to Trondheim in mid-northern Norway. The long overseas passage would be hazardous for single-engined aircraft and they would have little reserves of fuel. It was decided that a Mosquito, with its two man crew and specialized Gee navigational equipment, was needed to shepherd them across. Knowing that my friends in our Norwegian squadron had recently flown home to Oslo and were likely to be throwing some good parties, I unselfishly volunteered for the task. However the new Group Captain clearly (and rightly) suspected my motives.

' Now look here, Foxley-Norris, I realize there is likely to be a considerable shortage of fuel and a general disorganization at Trondheim. But I know as well as you do that with drop-tanks your Mosquito carries enough fuel to make the return trip without refuelling. So I want to see you back here this evening or tomorrow at the latest. Understood?'

It was understood, but I got a lucky break. Shortly before reaching Trondheim as we were flying over the Norwegian coast, one of the Spitfire pilots reported engine failure and an inevitable forced landing. I led the rest of the Wing to their destination and then in duty bound returned to conduct a square search to locate the downed pilot (as it turned out, he had been unwise enough to attempt a wheels-down forced landing in a forest clearing and had got away with it, finishing unhurt in his wingless cockpit in the middle of a wood). Having found him and directed search parties towards him, I returned to Trondheim. Imagine my chagrin when I discovered that this search flying had exhausted most of my fuel reserves; that there were not yet any replenishing facilities working at Trondheim; and that after all I had no alternative but to fly to Gaardemoen near Oslo to refuel. I respectfully signalled my intentions to base and flew south early the next morning.

May 1945 was abnormally hot and I landed at Gaardemoen in blazing sunshine. I was greeted by my Norwegian comrades, led by their Squadron Commander, Haakon Wenger, a rock hard, steel eyed man who had commanded by example and earned the respect rather than the affection of his men. I had expected to be taken straight into town but it was not to be.

Gaardemoen, like most Norwegian airfields, is surrounded by dense pine woods. In these woods the Germans had been accustomed to bury the victims of the Gestapo and the concentration camp, murdered hostages and tortured Resistance fighters; towards the end there had naturally been an upsurge of such resistance and the toll taken of them had been very heavy. Wenger insisted on my going with him to watch the Germans, now prisoners of war, disinter their late victims. One's every sense was appalled. The sight of disfigured, twisted bodies bound together often with barbed wire was matched only by the disgusting stench of decaying flesh and stale blood, and the buzzing of the mass of giant bluebottle flies that covered everything. Relentlessly Wenger conducted me round area after area of this dreadful shambles. At the very end he turned to me and said: ' Now, perhaps at last you will realize what war is really like. It is not a game, a sporting contest as you all seem to imagine. You English will never understand what war means until you see such things '.

It was a rebuke well earned and a lesson never forgotten. In later years when I commanded NATO air forces it was interesting to note that the Americans and the British, whose countries had never been occupied, found no problem in welcoming their new German allies and formed close and firm friendships with them, as indeed I did myself. Officers whose countries had known wartime occupation, and whose families had often been subjected to the suffering that it brought with it, naturally found initially very much more difficulty in establishing relationships other than strictly official and professional ones.

There was an amusing development in Oslo at about that time. A senior military member of the British ambassador's staff, who had better remain nameless to avoid libel suits, decided to give a prestige party to celebrate victory. Norway was at the time still on the verge of starvation and food was strictly rationed. Our hero thought he had detected at least a partial solution to the problem when he noted from the morning's bag that HMS So-and-So was in Copenhagen and would shortly weigh anchor for Oslo. The Captain was an old friend so the aspiring host signalled him, ' Looking forward to seeing you here. Please bring as much butter as you can '.

Things were apparently easier in Copenhagen so when the good ship So-and-So docked in Oslo, her manifest included no less than a quarter of a ton of butter consigned to the said military/diplomat, which caused no little stir. This reached the ears of the Ambassador, who rose in his wrath and decreed that the gentleman concerned should pay for the whole lot at the going inflated rate and then donate it to the Norwegian Red Cross. The eventual party proved rather a flop and the victuals were spartan.

On my return to Banff, I found news of an interesting development. Our late Commander in Chief, Sholto Douglas, had been translated from Coastal Command to British Air Forces (Germany). On arrival he cast a jaundiced eye around, disapproved of what he saw, and with typical tact announced that nobody out there had any idea of how to run a Mosquito squadron, and he intended to bring one over from his old Command to show the local lads how it ought to be done. One thing was painfully clear. Whoever was going to lead the squadron was going to be about as popular as a pork sausage in a mosque. Guess-who was inevitably the chosen victim for popular disapproval.

The difficulty of the appointment was accentuated by the fact that it carried with it the invidious responsibility of making a one-in-three selection from the aircrew of all the squadrons at Banff. A better way of losing friends I never encountered, and I managed to lose some, but in a few days had sorted out the best 20 crews available. In the circumstances they were, in the strictest sense, a picked bunch, perhaps one of the most highly qualified squadrons then serving. All were volunteers to go abroad with the squadron and we promptly applied ourselves to training ourselves to our new role. I even wrote a new song for the squadron (now renumbered No 14) to the tune of ' The Church's One Foundation '. One of its more repeatable verses ran:

> We were a Coastal Squadron
> From Trondheim to the Bay
> Although we didn't like it
> We flew all bloody day.
> But when we got to Germany
> We'll find that we're all right—
> Instead of all the bloody day
> We'll fly all bloody night.

I had the pleasure of singing this song again 15 years later when No 14 Squadron re-equipped with Phantoms under my overall command in Germany.

Training for our planned tasks and location was not confined to flying. Although at the time regulations against fraternizing with the conquered enemy were known to be strict I felt that it was basically undesirable to be taking to a foreign country people who had no knowledge of the language. I was lucky enough to find a qualified interpreter among my NCO pilots (not as surprising as it sounds in the light of their peacetime backgrounds) and put him to work. I was encouraged while passing the crew-room on several occasions to note the presence of a large and attentive class, but felt some unease when I discovered one evening written evidence of the theme of the day's lesson still chalked on the blackboard. It read: ' Wie viel kostet Ihre Schwester? '

In the event even this educational nugget was wasted, at least temporarily, for our initial destination on the Continent proved to be Cambrai in NE France—by coincidence the same area from which I had been evicted five years before.

After arrival there we settled down to the routine training of a Tactical Air Force Squadron. This included a detachment to an airfield close to Paris which I felt duty bound to lead in person; but the City of Light was still only beginning to recover from its wartime problems, there was much friction, bitterness and petty acts of grudge and outright vengeance. I encountered a number of hospitable pieces de Resistance, but on the whole one sensed a suspect atmosphere of many people trying to clamber on to that particular band-wagon without having worked their passage or earned their tickets.

On return to Cambrai, I found that the routine of training (we of course as ex-Coastal pilots had a lot to learn) was to be interrupted by some flying for a film. The film was to be based on the famous attack on Amiens prison, led by the great Pickard, himself one of the few casualties of the raid, and was to be called ' The Walls of Jericho '. I was invited to lead, somewhat unrealistically, a close formation of 24 Mosquitos; the cameras were sited on the perimeter of the airfield and, amongst other manoeuvres, we were to do a mass dive on them as if they were at the base of the walls of the prison. I wheeled my formation into position about five miles away, opened to nearly full throttle and began the mock attack. At about one mile from the target, with my faithful co-stars close around me, I sustained a complete seizure of my starboard engine, resulting in very sharp deceleration. The effect on the formation was startling; we went over the cameras in as tight a bunch of flying objects as could be seen outside a swarm of bees, only less organized.

The French director was ecstatic. Never had he seen such superb precision flying. How did we do it? The whole group seemed as if locked together (they damn nearly were). We adopted a becomingly traditionally British attitude of modesty, and accepted a great deal of free champagne; which we needed.

At the beginning of 1946 the squadron moved up to Gutersloh and I was transferred to a staff post in HQ 2 Group. The aftermath of the move from Cambrai produced one memorable incident.

The plan was to transfer the airfield back to the French Air Force, and a small rear party headed by three flight lieutenants was left in charge of the arrangements The idea was that British equipment should be removed, but the basic facilities handed over to the French. HQ No 2 Group dealt with the various processes and queries; one of the latter arrived in the form of a signal from the rear party, seeking instructions as to the future of the FIDO (Fog Intensive Dispersal Operation) equipment. This well publicised device had latterly been installed at a few selected Master airfields. It consisted of an elaborate and costly system of generators, control units, piping and pumps, which propelled pressurized kerosene into the air along both sides of the runway, ignited it and, by so doing, ' burned off ' the fog in the immediate area to allow aircraft to land. It was only used in emergency but was surprisingly effective; landing into it was like a voluntary descent into Dante's inferno, and a swing off the runway was inadvisable.

An overworked administrative staff officer, having ascertained that the master plan did not involve recovery of the FIDO equipment, signalled back ' Dispose of it '. In due course the French Air Force formally took over the airfield; and the three flight lieutenants who were ' wartime-only ' officers left successively the area, the country and the RAF. Shortly after the French re-occupation a convoy of heavy civilian trucks approached the aerodrome. Stopped at the guardroom, the passenger in the front explained that he was an important functionary in a large firm of local civil engineers; that they had recently purchased the FIDO equipment from ' les officiers anglais ' for a sum amounting to the equivalent of £150,000; that they had the documents to prove their ownership signed by the aforesaid ' officiers '; and had come to collect their lawful possessions.

A splendid Gallic fracas developed, whose ripples lapped eventually against Ministry walls in Paris and London. The three flight lieutenants concerned were traced and the majesty of the law loomed over them. However copies of the ' Dispose of it ' signals were blandly produced in justification and yet another complicated hassle brewed up. The outcome was that two of the flight lieutenants who lived in England were persuaded to disgorge what was left of their ill gotten gains on a promise of no further action. The third, from the safe distance of his home in the Canadian midwest, invited the authorities to do the other thing and got away with it.

Life in immediate postwar Germany proved artificial and somewhat dreary. Food was dull and still tightly rationed, as were cigarettes and spirits, though somehow or other there always seemed to be plenty to drink. While performing my air staff duties, I was pleased one day to receive a social visit from an ex-Flight Lieutenant Navigator from 143 Squadron. My enquiries disclosed that he was now commanding a small isolated unit which formed a component of the MRCP blind-bombing system; three such units at selected locations sent out triangulated intersecting signals to provide an accurate bomb-dropping point. There were only one other officer, two or three NCOs and a few airmen on the unit. I suggested it must be pretty dull.

' Not a bit of it, Sir ', he replied, ' we have a lot of fun and we do ourselves pretty well too—business with pleasure, as you might say. Talking of which, as I recall, you don't smoke cigarettes, do you, Sir? May I ask what you do with your ration of two hundred a week? '

' Oh, I just don't draw them—leave 'em for the heavy smokers.'

' That seems rather a waste if I may say so, Sir. Jolly good currency cigarettes are, you know—buy almost anything with them. You let me have your ration, Sir, and you'll be surprised what I can get you for them.'

' But that's black market, Colin.'

' Well, I suppose so. I look on it more as supply and demand, you see. They want 'em, we've got 'em. Anyway, you won't be involved yourself will you, if you just pass them on to me as an old friend? '

I was tempted and fell. I should have been ashamed of myself but the practice was very widespread and I asked myself why I should be about the only innocent for miles around. Two or three months later a nice, old-fashioned pocket watch reached me. My conscience tweaked me but I gave it a double gin to keep it quiet. A couple of weeks later all hell broke loose.

It transpired that my erstwhile comrade and his men had indeed been making themselves a little profit. But their business was not only black

75

market dealing—it was also armed robbery. Bored and underemployed, they had organized a nice little racket in holding up German village social functions at gun-point (Service revolvers were still generally issued) and relieving the participants of their jewellery and other portable possessions. I was in effect a fence. There was only one thing for it. I went round to the Provost Marshal and made a clean breast of it, naturally returning my one little bit of plunder. He gave me an almighty dressing down, but nothing more; and, as I left his office, I heard him roaring with laughter. My criminal associates did not get off so lightly.

I had another nasty experience with Service revolvers at about the same time. Officers' Mess accommodation at Gutersloh was quite inadequate, and the more senior of us, although bachelors, were billeted out in commandeered houses. I occupied a particularly baronial one with two fellow wing commanders and a group captain. One night I was awakened at about three in the morning by unmistakable noises downstairs. Grabbing and loading my revolver, I crept down and sure enough surprised a shadowy figure, loading a suitcase with valuables in the long dining room. I stood in the open double-doorway and shouted to him to put his hands up (I learnt later that I in fact called ' Hands off ', but it had the right effect). He came towards me with his hands raised, but as he got closer shoved one hand behind the open door and slammed it in my face, knocking me flat on my back. I staggered to my feet, furious at my stupidity, and swung the door open again. By then he was scrambling out of the window at the far end of the room. I fired off a couple of blind shots but he must have been at least 30 feet away and I am not a good shot, even in practice conditions and broad daylight. At least I had preserved our possessions, including our drink stocks with which the suitcase was largely packed.

The shots naturally roused the others in the house and they came rushing down. I told the story with some shame. We called the police and drove off round the darkened streets and up to the railway station on the off chance of catching him but had no luck; and, after a quick drink of our salvaged whisky, went back to bed.

A couple of hours later I was awoken by my batman with a cup of tea.

' Good morning, Sir, lovely morning. Oh, and there's a body in the garden.'

' A—what? '

' A body, Sir, down by the garden gate.'

I flung on some clothes, shouted to my friends and dashed outside. Down by the small gate (we had driven out by car earlier) was a dead man. He was shot so clean through the heart that I noticed he had scarcely bled at all; yet he had run a good dozen yards from the house. And he was in British airman's uniform.

It was a nasty moment indeed. I knew that the law only permitted a reasonable degree of violence in retaliation on these occasions. Shooting an unarmed burglar stone dead certainly did not come under that heading. However it was not long before it was discovered that the uniform was stolen; and that its wearer was a much wanted SS man on the run with a string of recent robberies and assaults to his discredit. My friends, and indeed my superiors later, were free with their congratulations, but they did not seem to be appropriate. It is not an episode about which I felt then or ever since any sense of pride.

As staff officers we kept our hand in flying Mosquitos from Gutersloh and I was also initiated into the unique joys of gliding, at which I later became a qualified instructor: and flew my first jet aircraft, a Meteor 4. Gutersloh was an airfield we had taken over practically lock, stock and barrel from the Luftwaffe who had used it mostly as a night-fighter training unit. It was built in typically heavy, baroque style and included among its amenities a Bierkeller and also a small low-ceilinged card room, seating about eight people at the top of a tower which formed part of the officers' mess. One evening we were sitting around the table there, drinking and gossiping and playing poker, when one of the players (perhaps trying to palm an ace) discovered what appeared to be a bell-push under the edge of the table. He pressed it experimentally and to his and everybody's astonishment one of the main ceiling beams, apparently hinged, bent creakingly in the middle and descended slowly and precisely on the head of someone sitting opposite.

An explanation had to be found for this extraordinary phenomenon and was forthcoming from one of the German mess staff who had been kept on from the old days. The story was that, two or three years before, the base had been commanded by a great fighter ace, who in his cups became greater still and around the same table had night after night regaled his juniors with increasingly improbable tales of his exploits in the Battle of Britain and elsewhere. When they were bold enough to question his claim, for example, to have shot down 16 Spitfires in one day, his invariable reply was ' I swear it. If it is not true, may the ceiling fall on my head '.

So the next time they arranged that it should. Perhaps they had more sense of humour than we gave them credit for.

It was with mixed feelings that I heard shortly afterwards that I was to go on the next Staff College course, in the autumn of 1946. From a career angle it was good news, but it meant my first real break from the world of flying; and it also meant demotion to my substantive rank of Squadron Leader. This was quite a common fate at the time, some unfortunates having to come down two ranks, but that did not make it any more palatable or explicable to one's mystified and suspicious elderly female relatives (' Not another court-martial, dear? '). There was a bizarre custom in Germany at the time to celebrate such occasions by a Demotion Dinner Party, which comprised an ordinary dinner menu served in reverse, starting with port, coffee and cigars and finishing hours later with consomme and dry Martinis. It was even less enjoyable than it sounds.

I duly gave mine, and departed for England with indigestion and a hang-over.

11 Dual Control

I completed the short Staff College Course then in vogue without difficulty; received the now routine rebuke for light heartedness from my masters; and considered the immediate future. The great majority to graduate from the College at that time were sent to the Air Ministry, since the latter was being hurriedly vacated by ' hostilities only ' officers returning to their original professions. It so happened that for domestic reasons it would suit me to go to London; my mother had converted a small house into flats and the first floor tenant had to share bathroom etc. with her own ground floor flat. I was the obvious man to do this; at the same time to conduct some supervision on her behalf; and to gain some professionally valuable staff experience at the same time.

I volunteered for the Air Ministry, alone among my fellow students. 60 per cent of the latter went unwillingly to the Ministry. I was not among them. I should have learnt about volunteering by then.

Instead I was sent a few miles up the road as ' Flying Training 1 ' at HQ Reserve Command at White Waltham. The job was lightly loaded and enjoyable since I was responsible for the activities of the Auxiliary Squadrons and the University Air Squadrons, both home grounds to me. A number of my contemporaries and friends were on hand to pass the time. We were poorly housed and poorly paid, but as bachelors we managed to enjoy ourselves; and to keep fit we played squash, golf and cricket.

The latter was to be my Nemesis. Village cricket has always been one of my chief delights and remains so to this day. We had something better still, in the shape of a local pub which had its own cricket-ground and ran its own side, impartially selected from patrons of the saloon and public bars. It was in the former that I met and later fell in love with a very beautiful woman. Our feelings developed mutually, but unhappily she proved to be the wife of a good friend, who was also my cricket captain. A genuine crisis of emotion and conflict of loyalties arose, but fortunately they were resolved when it proved that his affections were also engaged elsewhere. During the ensuing winter the matter was brought to an amicable conclusion and appropriate rearrangements made.

The only residual complication was that during the same period my friend and his new wife were posted elsewhere, and I took on the job of cricket captain, my wife acting as hostess. This produced considerable confusion in the minds of the captains of visiting teams (one heard whispered asides ' Surely?—isn't it the same? D'you suppose she's sort of ex-officio? ' and so on).

We too were in for a move. The RAF at the time must have had thousands of recently demoted officers, and without false modesty one must concede that luck played a considerable part in one's chances of re-emerging from the mass. Fortunately luck was on my side.

I was sitting at my desk at the HQ one day, doing no obvious harm to anyone, when a file was brought in, with a minute addressed to Flying Training 1. It was a long and wordy minute, which in summary stated that a vacancy was about to arise for the appointment of Wing Commander commanding the Oxford University Air Squadron; that the qualifications were so and so and such and such, including preferably being an ex-member of the Squadron; since my present appointment brought me into close and regular contact with University Air Squadrons, their problems and special requirements etc, etc, etc, did I know of and could I recommend anybody suitably qualified? I replied as follows:

SPSO
Reference your minute 14/112/1/UAS of 21 July 1948.
   (a) yes
   (b) me

                      C. N. Foxley-Norris
                      Sqn Ldr FT1

Perhaps surprisingly, it worked. Shortly thereafter my bride and I were installed on Boar's Hill near Oxford, with my Wing Commander's stripe newly restored.

It was a very happy period. Professionally, I had few problems. The link between University and Squadron had always been close and remained so. The University authorities valued their Squadron and were proud of it and supported its CO in many ways. The undergraduates were in many cases ex-Servicemen and therefore more mature and responsible than one might normally have expected; though I sometimes had occasion to doubt this, as when John Lawrence (now Lord Oaksey) flung an empty Chianti bottle out of his car and through the windscreen of my own following one. The Squadron was heavily oversubscribed with a long waiting list, so I had few disciplinary problems since everyone knew that his place could easily be filled. My staff was led by Squadron Leader Jack Acres (Sergeant Acres when I first joined the squadron) and Miss Olive Round, the Secretary, who between them had served OUAS for nearly 50 years, and guided my novice steps through various intricate local mazes.

It may be thought that the command of a University Air Squadron was somewhat of a backwater; rightly, perhaps, but this was a good time to be in a backwater. The RAF, like the other Services, was going through a difficult and unhappy period. The vast if essential postwar cuts were scarcely finished when the urgent and rushed build up for Korea followed. It was an awkward, typical time of postwar malaise, aimless at best, disillusioned at worst. A few picked individuals found something worthwhile to do. Teddy Donaldson and his fellows set world speed records and developed the fledgling techniques of jet combat. The problems of high speed, high altitude operations and the possibilities of supersonic flight were explored; though our national attitude to the latter was deplorably craven, based on wildly inaccurate scientific advice, and we thereby lost much of the advantage which our pioneering in jet-propulsion had brought us. But on the whole it was a depressing and stagnant time—a good time to be punting gently in the quiet backwaters of Academe.

Domestically, it was also of course a happy time. My wife, showing the adaptability which later proved one of her most admirable qualities, made the switch from a khaki to a light-blue environment without apparent difficulty. We entertained as far as our narrow means allowed, both new friends and old friends, of whom I had many round Oxford. I had been made a temporary member of the Senior Common Room of my old College, Trinity, and repaired to the SC stores to buy a bottle of port for our first dinner-party.

' Yes, Sir ', said the cellarer, ' we are serving the Cockburn '27 at present '.

' Oh, I'm sorry, Tom ', I confessed, ' I'm afraid I was thinking in terms of something like twenty-five bob a bottle at most '.

' The '27, Sir ', he replied, ' is fifteen shillings the bottle '.

We drank a great deal of port thereafter. This and other minor consolations made life very tolerable. Now that I am an Honorary Fellow of the College they are again open to me. We later moved to Witney and it was there that, to the best of my knowledge, I invented the slipped disc.

This affliction is by now of course a household word, having perhaps passed even beyond the fashionable to the outmoded phase. In 1949 this was not the case. If you had a ' bad back ' you rubbed it with Elliman's Embrocation or took Kruschen's Salts (' Every picture tells a story '). One morning I found while sitting in the bath that I could only raise my right leg two or three inches without causing excruciating pain down the sciatic nerve. Having tried both Messrs Elliman's and Kruschen's product without success, I took the offending member along to the Radcliffe Infirmary, eschewing the available RAF medical services who would probably have taken me off flying. It was here that the fatal words ' slipped disc ' or more professionally ' prolapsed intervertebral disc ' first reached my consciousness, and unfortunately they have haunted me ever since, with varying degrees of distressfulness and intensity.

Perhaps the most dramatic instance occurred a couple of years later. I was by then on the Directing Staff of the RAF Staff College at Bracknell and we were renting a particularly damp and cramped converted stables at Ascot. One morning I rose from the matrimonial couch, turned on and lit the gas fire and, still leaning on the mantelpiece, reached down to pull on a sock. At that moment it felt as if somebody had torn out my sciatic nerve by the roots. I screamed (for lack of a nicer word). My wife, aroused, shot up in bed and fainted. It was not until the pain from my scorching left leg exceeded that from the nerve that I fell away from the fire.

Help duly arrived, and I was carted off to hospital with the interesting and I suspect unique diagnosis of ' Severely prolapsed intervertebral disc; first degree burns of the left leg; and shock '. In the circumstances the last was perhaps understandable.

However I nevertheless remain qualified for full flying duties for a further 25 years, off and on.   While I was still commanding the OUAS we were based at Kidlington, where the Air Commodore commanding the Maintenance Unit, also had back trouble.   He was an officer of the Equipment (non-flying) Branch but his injuries were genuinely attributable to wartime service, having been sustained in a very nasty Jeep accident during the fighting in Italy.   Consequently, when he retired, he was able to claim quite a considerable portion of his pension free of tax, the contemporary means of compensation for such injuries.   A year or two later, he received a really delightful letter from an Air Ministry official, more or less along these lines:

Dear Air Commodore,

I write in connection with your approved drawing of an element of tax-free pension, attributable to wartime injuries suffered to your back.

We here feel that you have a decision to make.   Either you may continue to draw that well-earned tax-free element; or you may continue to ride in Point-to-Point races (incidentally, congratulations on your last two victories of which we were pleased to learn from the *Telegraph*); but not, we would suggest, both.

The choice is of course entirely yours.

Yours etc etc

I should much like to have met that official.   The Air Commodore prudently gave up his racing.

We left Oxford with regret and I spent an enjoyable and professionally rewarding two and a half years as an instructor at Bracknell.   One of the pleasanter aspects of such an appointment is that nearly three hundred of one's juniors pass through one's hands, and thereafter one almost always finds a familiar face in any service environment (though by now their names always escape me).   At that time I re-met Lord Dowding for the first time since 1940.   It was on the occasion of the annual garden party and I was playing cricket for the Staff College.   I always fondly imagined he might recall me as one of The Few; but whenever we met thereafter until his death, it was always, ' Foxley-Norris?   Oh, yes!   You're the man who nearly killed me with a cricket ball when I was sitting in a deck-chair at Bracknell '.   I suppose it's nice to be remembered for something.

During our stay at Bracknell, I made the first of a catalogue of disastrous ventures into the housing market.   A good deal of work was being done at the time to provide acceptable housing by cutting up large houses into slices like a wedding cake, and selling them as separate units.   I managed to raise the down payment on a mortgage of a small and indeed humble part of a large Edwardian mansion at Ascot, called Queen's Hill; the price asked was very high, but this was attributable to the fact that it enjoyed a private entrance onto the Golden Mile, which would produce high rentals during Ascot Week.   While we were surveying our abode, the late head gardener of the estate, a most courteous gentleman of the old school, approached and introduced himself.

' I understand that you have purchased a portion of the house, Sir.'

' Yes, indeed, Mr Quiller—the rear end of the westerly wing. I believe it was originally the servants' quarters? '

' The west wing, Sir? Oh, no! That would be the *footmen's* quarters.'

Inevitably it had to be christened ' Flunkeys '. But the outcome was unhappy. In 1953 I proceeded to the Far East to defend the Empire; and during my absence some villain moved the Golden Mile (Golden Gates and all). Apparently the original ' Mile ' was in fact some distance short of a statute mile, and therefore times clocked over it did not count for the records. The solution was to convert its first half into a long sweeping curve. In the process I lost my precious private entrance and, as a result, much of my money. I enquired later of my man of business whether there might be anybody I could sue for recompense.

' Well, you might try the Duke of Norfolk ', he replied, ' but I don't suppose it would do much good '.

I accepted his advice and chalked up to experience what proved to be the first of many such misadventures. It is by now a matter of record that in business matters everything I touch turns to lead. In housing I sold freeholds in Kensington and Greece in 1970, both of which trebled in value the following year. In investment I broke the Australian market in the autumn of 1968, purchasing incidentally Broken Hill Proprietary at the highest price ever recorded; a couple of year later I broke Bernie Cornfield and his IOS, perhaps my most dramatic achievement in this field; and my modest entry into the stock market in the winter of 1972 produced a fall in all shares which bade fair to exceed that of 1929 (I was too young to be held responsible for that, otherwise I have no doubt I would be).

This facility has now, after retirement, led me to consider setting up ' Losers Incorporated '. The modus operandi would be for myself and colleagues, whose sole qualifications would be, like mine, an unbroken track record of business failure, to await the announcement of the launching of a major share issue, say by ICI or GEC. We would then contact them formally to ascertain how much they would be prepared to pay for Losers Inc not to buy in; for if we did the issue would inevitably fall flat on its face. After a couple of unhappy experiences, the business world would get the point and all would go as merry as a wedding bell—at least for Losers Inc.

I am assured that this is not blackmail. It is called counter-consultancy. If any reader is interested, and of course can prove his own qualifications, please contact me.

12 *East of Suez*

I awaited my posting from the Bracknell staff with unusual interest. Although my command of the Oxford University Air Squadron had been classed as a flying appointment, the Chipmunk had been scarcely a demanding aircraft, and at Bracknell one's flying had been routine and spare time although I did manage to crash a Spitfire en passant. Only one other incident in my log-book at the time may be worth recording.

A good friend of mine at Bracknell, Bernard Chacksfield, had gone off to sail in a cross-Channel race. He was overdue back at Hamble after encountering very light winds but his general whereabouts and estimated time of return could be calculated. I went over to our local airfield at White Waltham, where I had an Anson booked to do some continuation flying. There I met some Air Training Corps cadets from the Eton contingent hanging about in the hope of a flight, which they were fully entitled to do. I corralled a couple of them and set them to planning a navigational exercise. I explained the probable course and location of the yacht and told them to work out a timed flight plan to intercept it. This would be useful training for them as potential aircrew.

They came up with an answer which appeared sensible and we set off. I had told them that the yacht should be easily recognisable by its unusual characteristic of white foresails and a tan mainsail. As we coasted out over the Needles the visibility began to deteriorate in low cloud and haze. My earnest amateur navigators worked on their drifts and wind-speeds and passed me alterations of course but I was privately pretty pessimistic of our prospects. Unexpectedly, however, after about a further half-hour's flying, there she was, half a mile dead ahead of us. My crew were as delighted as I was astonished, and we went down and beat up the boat and its occupants, who waved their arms in excitement and apparent welcome as we conducted a number of very low passes over them before turning for base.

My cadets went off back to school, full of the wonders of navigation and their own prowess at it. Well pleased, I returned to Bracknell, but was taken somewhat aback to find Bernard Chacksfield tucking into a hearty lunch there. He had apparently got in early that morning and was well on his way home by train at the time of our epic navigational feat.

If the crew of the yacht concerned by any chance read this, I offer them a belated apology—but they *did* have the same unusual colour-mixture of sails.

This sort of thing apart, however, one's flying was pretty routine and I had high hopes of returning to a front-line unit. It was therefore with some disappointment that I learnt that my next posting was to be as the Air Planner at HQ Far East Air Force. When I protested about another paper-pushing job, I was rightly told that I should consider myself lucky, because that was 'where the action was'. This indeed was true, because the communist terrorist campaign in Malaya was at its height, as was the fighting in Korea; and there were wars and rumours of wars all over the area, notably in French Indo-China (as it was then), Taiwan, the Philippines and so on. My protests were overridden, for which I have ever since been grateful since this period proved one of the most interesting and rewarding of my career, and initiated a personal association with the Far East which has played a large part in my life ever since.

I flew out to Singapore alone in the scheduled Hastings aircraft; my wife, who had recently undergone an operation, was to follow me a few weeks later. My own flight was uneventful; hers proved more interesting. While she was recovering at my mother's home, the Air Ministry contacted her and asked if she would be kind enough to escort and chaperone the young fiancee of a sergeant serving in Singapore. The girl was on her first flight and would be the only other female passenger on the flight. Slightly mystified my wife explained that she herself was convalescent, but would help out in any way possible.

When the two met at the departure airfield the mystery was resolved since it became immediately apparent that the young lady in question was at least eight months' pregnant. It was to be a race between the stork and the Hastings, the latter notoriously a slow mover and the former equally an unpredictable starter. My wife's anxieties on her companion's behalf were accentuated by the extreme bumpiness of the flight, conducted largely at medium altitude over desert and mountain; and by the fact that at each of several stops en route, a posse of fellow-NCOs, clearly forewarned, carried off the young lady to the Sergeants' Mess and rendered her even fuller than Nature had already done; and, more intensely perhaps, by the rumour, well founded at the time, that Hastings aircraft in rough weather were shedding their tail-planes in all directions.

However the ending was a happy one; the cargo, human and otherwise, was delivered undisturbed at Changi; a white wedding attended by my wife as a sort of midwife manquée followed in a day or two; and a bouncing (and legitimate) boy duly arrived the following week. All swell that end's well, as one might say.

We ourselves settled down quickly and happily in Singapore, both personally and professionally. Since we had no children and no record of separated service, we were faced with a long wait for a married quarter; so decided to live in Singapore town itself. This involved me in a 45-minute drive to and from work at Changi but was worth it on balance. Married-quarter life has its advantages but also its drawbacks, one of which is a tendency to become isolated from the general society in which one is living. This is particularly to be regretted when that society is as novel, as fascinating and as educative as that of the great cosmopolitan city of Singapore. One of the real attractions offered to the regular Serviceman was to travel to and live in such places, although the opportunities are sadly now much reduced. To spend one's time abroad in a sort of British uniformed ghetto is thoroughly deplorable and, in the strictest sense, wasteful. Unfortunately there are financial temptations, and even on occasion compulsions, to do so. I was to encounter the same situation years later when I became Commander in Chief of RAF Germany.

We solved our own accommodation problem in a novel way. At that time the expatriate big businessmen of Singapore, the Tuan Besars or Number Ones of the great commercial houses and their families used to take regular long leaves to Britain or sometimes Australia. Because passage was usually by boat this involved absences of six months or more, during which time their large houses were empty and vulnerable, and their equally large domestic staffs idle. A respectable senior Service officer and wife were welcome housekeeper/tenants and in most cases all we had to pay for living in more than oriental splendour was the staff wages. The two snags were the constant moves we had to make, which however offered few problems without children, pets or similar encumbrances; and the fact that, with numerous and highly efficient servants available, my wife began to find time lying heavy on her always energetic hands.

This latter problem she solved by taking a job as a ground hostess with Qantas, the Australian airline for whose trunk-line aircraft Singapore was a regular stop-over. On paper, this was a fairly straightforward and un-complicated commitment, involving twice a week sessions of meeting an evening aircraft, making overnight arrangements for the passengers and seeing them off the following morning. Unhappily, the punctuality of the Constellation aircraft left much to be desired, and our social life became confused and occasionally hectic.

She met a lot of interesting celebrities en passant, and some fascinating human beings among the less well known. This was the period of large scale Government-sponsored immigration to Australia, particularly from Eastern Europe. Many of the less sophisticated travellers from the latter had been apparently accustomed to meet the winter cold by donning most of their wardrobes for its duration. Faced with emigration and lacking hand baggage, they often solved the problem by wearing all their remaining clothes as well for the flight. The results in the steaming hot climate of Singapore were unpleasant both for themselves and their close escorts. One particular Bulgarian gentleman drew some attention when he solved the problem of formal dinner wear in the hallowed halls of Raffles Hotel by stripping down to his pyjamas. Life for a ground hostess was never dull.

My own professional activities were also of remarkable interest. Pri-marily, I was concerned with the air planning of the counter-terrorist opera-tions in Malaya, occasionally managing to grab the opportunity to take an active part in them myself. There were many lessons to be learnt.

In the first place, the environment of our activity offered obstacles and difficulties which made the application of the normally accepted techniques of air power unrealistic. The enemy was effectively unidentifiable; he was of course indigenous, usually Chinese (but then nearly half the population of Malaya was Chinese); he wore no uniform and did his best to merge with the civilian population; and the dense jungle and mountains which constituted practically the whole of the area of operations provided total cover against air observation, visual or photographic, this accentuated by the extremely bad climatic conditions that generally prevailed, low cloud, mist and thunderstorms with extreme turbulence and blinding monsoon rain.

In the face of all this we still attempted to provide offensive support for our soldiers along the established lines of World War II. We dropped great tonnages of bombs, often on area targets of considerable size. These bombs eventually had to be especially delay-fused so as not to explode harmlessly on impact with the canopy of jungle foliage, often more than 100 feet above the ground. Even when the bombs did explode at ground level, their blast was largely absorbed by the jungle. On one exceptional occasion however we scored a surprising success. A guerilla force had been reasonably accurately located and heavy bombs were aimed at them. One of these blew up what must have been the biggest red ant-heap in Malaya. Its enraged denizens attacked the guerillas with blinding fury, driving them out into the open and into the grateful arms of our waiting troops.

Cannon and rocket-fire proved even less effective since they were almost entirely absorbed by the jungle canopy. Indeed the only established result of this activity was a sharp complaint from the Malaya lumbering industry of heavy damage to their saws, attributed to the fact that many of the tree-trunks proved to be full of metal, indubitably inserted by the Royal Air Force.

Another unfortunate aspect of the air operations was the re-equipment of the Far East Air Force coincidentally with the height of the security operation. The piston-engined Lincoln bombers and Hornet fighter-ground attack aircraft were replaced by the jet-propelled Canberra and Venom. Although the speed and general performance of the new aircraft were naturally much better, for the job in hand they were inferior to the aircraft they succeeded for example in weapon-load and, most importantly, in endurance, particularly at low-level. In saying this, I offer no criticism of the decision to re-equip, for it exemplified a problem that in those days (and to some extent even today) faced the RAF and to a lesser degree any other air force, ie they were faced with a continuing prospect of having to fight two alternative sorts of war; major war against a powerful, sophisticated well equipped enemy, and minor war of a policing or peace keeping nature against smaller, less developed but nevertheless often awkward opponents.

The former type of warfare called for aircraft and weapons systems of the highest sophistication and performance (and therefore cost) to meet the quality and quantity of the potential enemy's forces. To use such aircraft and weapons against minor enemies was to crack a walnut with a sledge hammer—and a gold-plated one at that. The problem was that we could not afford both a thoroughbred classic horse and a useful hack. We dare not forego the former, for on it the survival of our nation might one day depend. Therefore we had to forego the latter; and consequently found ourselves with unsuitable weapons to fight small battles and minor wars.

The point can perhaps best be illustrated by an incident some years later. In 1963 there was friction and a possibility of conflict between a Latin American state (let us call it Xanadia) and one of our then remaining colonies in the area. In appreciating the local military balance, a Foreign office paper offered the comment ' The Xanadian airforce is handicapped by being equipped with World War II aircraft, the P-51 Mustang and the A-26 Invader bomber '. Against which I, as then Assistant Chief of Defence Staff, wrote, rudely but accurately, ' Nonsense. These are the ideal aircraft for the job. I wish we had some '.

All this is not to say that air power was ineffective in Malaya. Quite the reverse. It in fact made a most telling contribution to victory but in an unexpected way, ie not by offensive support, reconnaissance or air defence but by providing the priceless gifts of flexibility, mobility and logistic self-sufficiency to troops who would otherwise have been much handicapped in this respect vis-a-vis their opponents. The Malayan Communist-Terrorist was a guerilla in the truest sense of the word, indigenous and thoroughly conversant with every aspect of his environment, lightly armed and living off the land, unencumbered with supply or organization and astonishingly fast-moving through apparently impenetrable jungle. Our own troops were alien to the environment, and the climate, initially undertrained in the role, overloaded with gear and equipment and almost immobilized at ground level by the jungle and its life, unfamiliar, frightening and almost impassable. Furthermore the enemy always seemed to know exactly where they were and either ambushed them or vanished. Air transport resolved almost all these problems. Our troops, moving at perhaps a half of the rate of their enemies at ground level, could be moved at fifty times their speed above the jungle canopy by helicopter or by short take-off and landing aircraft; once moved they could be provided with all they needed by supply dropping aircraft in their new location or even on the march. The tortoise became the hare without losing any of its endurance; the guerilla, faced with an enemy who had accelerated from a stumbling front-row forward to a lightning and elusive wing three-quarter, finally conceded defeat. Of course, there were innumerable other factors that contributed to that defeat; but few that had such a dramatic and telling effect.

The fascinating thing about a life in military aviation is that there is always something new to be learnt. There are two basic and apparently paradoxical principles to be applied. Never forget the lessons of the past. Never re-apply them too rigidly to new circumstances. Either way disaster lies.

In the autumn of 1955, I was sitting around in Singapore getting on with my interesting job and feeling pretty satisfied with the way things had been going in Malaya. At short notice I was instructed to accompany General Sixsmith, the Chief of Staff to the Far East Land Forces, to Washington. We were to pick up the Joint Planners from London en route. The object of the exercise was to consider at the highest level and with all urgency what the Americans and ourselves might be able to do to prevent the fall of Dien Bien Phu, the beleaguered Vietnam key-point where the French were coming under unbearable pressure. The immediacy of their need was such that air power must inevitably play a leading part in any plans we produced.

We arrived in Washington early on a Saturday morning, went straight to the underground caverns of the Pentagon and into conference with our

American colleagues. After two days of ceaseless effort, we produced a plan, based largely on the heavy bombing of the perimeter of and approaches to the encircled French position. We were not particularly confident of the prospects of our plan, but it offered the only realistic option open to us in the time scale.

Early on the Tuesday morning an extremely high-powered conference assembled in a large hall. The American team was led by Generals Grunther (in the chair) and Ridgeway, our own by Field Marshal Harding, each accompanied by a bevy of high ranking airmen. We humble planners assembled at the far end of the table and consideration and discussion of our proposals began. After a while, a door halfway down the hall opened, and a young officer bearing a piece of paper entered and looked somewhat nervously about him.

' Over here, son! ' called General Ridgeway, ' Let's see what you have there '.

The paper was handed over, opened and read. It seemed to be quite short. After a moment's study, the General deliberately re-folded it and looked around him.

' Gentlemen ', he announced, ' I regret to have to inform you that Dien Bien Phu has fallen '.

So we all packed up and went home. For some reason it has stuck in my mind that my return fare from Singapore had cost the taxpayer £637.

The ill wind of the French débâcle in Vietnam at least produced a prompt reaction from many countries with interests in the area, that the defence of those interests must be co-ordinated. In due course the South East Asia Treaty Organization was established, with its headquarters in Bangkok and with an initial membership consisting of the United States, Great Britain, France, Pakistan, Thailand, the Philippines, Australia and New Zealand.

Such a large and widely spread organization called for considerable military planning activity, in turn involving a lot of travel. The whole basic strategy, the aims, contingency plans and contributions had to be evolved, papers written and conferences held. In the interval we had brought our conflict in Malaya to a successful conclusion, so my own professional energies were largely re-channelled to SEATO activity. It was all very interesting and absorbing in the early stages, although later one could not help wondering whether China's derisory description of the Organization as a "paper tiger" did not contain some truth: there was undoubtedly a lot of paper about.

The staff and planners soon got to know each other well and learnt to work in a spirit of general co-operation, with only occasional instances of awkwardness or friction. One factor that did not help matters was the traditional meanness of the British Treasury when applied to travel expenses. Wing Commanders and other such underlings were only entitled to second-class or tourist facilities on airlines. We were used to this contemptuous treatment, but it became embarrassing when SEATO planners travelled en bloc, since all the other nations' representatives (even the comparatively impoverished New Zealanders) travelled first-class, with the usual free drinks and prerequisites; and the poor old British sat up front and enjoyed pack-lunches and orange squash. Kindly little brown hands could be observed passing forward glasses of champagne when the stewardesses weren't looking.

The British Army and the Air Force authorities were apparently content to accept this treatment of their representatives. Not so the Royal Navy, God bless them, whose Commander in Chief in the Far East was that outstanding character Admiral Sir Charles Lamb. In direct, seamanlike language he told the financiers what they could do with their regulations. Officers of the Royal Navy were not, repeat not, to be embarrassed or humi-liated in international eyes and would travel first-class with their colleagues. Splendid; but unfortunately his army and air force colleagues were made of less stern stuff. So we finished up with the interesting spectacle of all the other national staffs and our own navy colleagues travelling first-class; and the colonels and wing-commanders continuing to slum it. All very good for morale and the international image.

We did not always travel in civilian aircraft, but the military alternatives tended to be even more austere. On one occasion, a fellow RAF officer and myself set course for a SEATO conference in Hawaii. The rendezvous was attractive but the journey of several thousand miles in slow, noisy military transports, with several refuelling stops, much less so. Our first stage ended at Clarke Field outside Manila in the Philippines. There we were lavishly entertained by the USAF at the Officers' Club, so that when we were called in the early hours for our dawn take-off we seemed to have only been in bed for a matter of minutes—indeed we had only been so, and were in no fit state to leave it.

We staggered to the waiting truck and down to the airfield where we were greeted by the unattractive spectacle of the ancient US Navy DC4 which was to carry us to the next stop at Guam. The trip was due to take ten hours or more; the flight plan promised us a turbulent ride through the inter-tropical front; and, the aircraft was rigged fore and aft with parachutist-type seats of extreme discomfort. A compassionate WAVE airhostess approached us as we huddled into them.

'Good morning, gentlemen. Why, you gentlemen certainly don't look too good this lovely morning.'

'Madam, we feel even worse than we look. Is there anything you can do for us?'

'Well—as a matter of fact there is, although I surely shouldn't do it.' You see, we're allowed to hand out these pills for airsickness. They're just a heavy sedative and the maximum dose I'm supposed to give is two. But I'll just slip you four each, and you won't know a thing for four or five hours—then maybe you'll be feeling a little better'.

We accepted with profound gratitude, gulped down our double ration and, as predicted, passed happily and readily into profound slumber. Alas! the best laid plans of even SEATO planners can go the way of those of mice and men. Our ancient vehicle crawled to the end of the runway, lumbered into the air, promptly lost an engine and returned thankfully to terra firma via a quick circuit of the airfield.

' Sorry, folk, have to line up another aircraft, I guess ', crackled the intercom. ' Everybody out, please.'

Everybody, that is, except for two deplorably, irrevocably inert Wing Commanders who had to be hauled out like sacks of wheat, practically frog-marched over to the hangar in the now blazing sun, and propped against the wall; where they sank quietly and imperceptibly to the ground and continued their slumbers.

The moral must be that, if you must go on the pill, make sure you are fully committed and there is a real need before you do so.

Professionally, as I hope I have demonstrated, life had a great deal to offer. Personally, it was just as full and varied; but before proceeding to describe these attractions I might take the opportunity to make an interim survey of some aspects of the Royal Air Force during the ten post-war years.

The first few years were of course predictably traumatic. By 1948, nine out of ten of those serving on VE-day had left; many were downgraded not only in rank, as I described earlier, but in status and self-esteem (sergeant pilots with DFM's drove ration trucks or clerked in the stores), so morale suffered and discontent was rife; those who left were replaced by reluctant, disinterested conscripts; and the whole atmosphere was one of aimlessness and uncertainty, natural but nevertheless unhappy. Those who stayed in often envied those who had moved on.

By 1949 the Berlin air lift had proved the malaise temporary and the core still sound (my only personal contribution to this historic programme was to be blown upside down in a Tiger Moth at Abingdon by an urgently-taxying, coal-filled Hastings aircraft). Korea and our national participation in the United Nations force deployed to fight there gave us further sense of purpose; and the Malayan operations largely completed the cure. But all was still not well in the Royal Air Force of the mid-1950s.

The life blood of any military service is the quality of its men. Weapons and weapon-systems change, develop and dissolve. The man is the essential factor and most essential among the men is the leader. Each of the British Services has known periods when the highest standards of leadership were not maintained, eg the Army in the Crimea. This was also true of the Royal Air Force of the time of which I write.

There were various reasons. The tide of war had receded and carried with it many of our best. Most, alas! had gone to their graves—it was difficult to build a postwar air force on its foundation stone of Cranwell when some of its prewar courses, the élite of the Service, had sustained nearly 100 per cent casualties. Others, like Lord Portal, Sholto Douglas, Max Aitken, Douglas Bader, decided to move into commerce, industry or the professions. Doubly therefore there were gaps to be filled and not all were adequately filled. Some new holders of high rank had little if any combat experience, often through no fault of their own. In consequence they did not always enjoy the confidence of their subordinates and, worse still, often lacked confidence in themselves. A contributing factor to this situation was the otherwise welcome expansion of the armed forces that followed developments in Korea. Those who had been trying to persuade themselves, and others, that all was now for the best in the best of possible worlds, and that we had no need for national fire insurance because fire had been outlawed, had been compelled by public opinion to agree to repair and strengthen the defences they had been undermining. The re-provision of forces called for more men and more leaders. The supply situation for the latter had been weakened as I described above. As a result at all levels for a while men were promoted higher than their quality and talents merited.

On the other side of the coin, some of the genuinely great and glamorous men of war still served, Embry, Broadhurst, and their like at somewhat lower levels. Round such men there tended to accumulate, like iron filings round a magnet, cliques, empires, circuses, call them what you will. One was an 'Embry boy' or one was not. If one was not, one's immediate prospects were lessened. If one was, the immediate prospect was bright, but when one's master finally departed, one feared the wolves would pounce; and they did. It was all much exaggerated; but it was inherently undesirable and most people were relieved when it all died away as the years passed. I personally, like many others, viewed with concern a later tendency for it to revive.

Apart from such temporary and internal local difficulties, the enemy without was always at our gates. No, not the dreaded denizens of Russia or Germany; more the even more traditional enemy of our military establishment, the men from Whitehall. Abetted by pusillanimous and sometimes dishonest politicians they had between the wars so cribbed, cabined and confined our defence expenditure and consequently our defence capability, that only a panic re-armament at the eleventh hour, assisted by some classic midjudgments by the Germans, precariously contrived our national survival. As soon as the war was over these men of the Treasury, the Civil Service Department and so on resumed their self-appointed task of eroding the country's security. The revival consequent upon Korea and Malaya came as an unwelcome setback to them, but they rightly assessed it as only temporary. Within weeks, for example, of the successful completion of the Malayan emergency, I found myself on behalf of my Commander in Chief writing a desperate paper to counter a proposal to abolish his long-range reconnaissance force. The fact that the lack of such an effective force probably contributed more to the loss of Singapore in 1942 than any other single factor had apparently escaped the notice of our home-based Abominable No-men.

We won that one; but there was always another front to be faced, another insidious whittler to be detected and deterred. It was a messy and nasty business and many men of good-heart finally sickened of it and sought their occupation elsewhere.

That little burst of indignation must not, however, persuade the reader that life was intolerable or even unpleasant in the Services of the time. It was not as good as it could have been, but for me at least the pros still far outweighed the cons. In the Far East particularly there was so much all around to delight and enchant that any professional discontents that existed could easily be survived.

13 The Chinese are Different

As I noted above, one of the minor tragedies of overseas service is how many people turn in on themselves and their military environment and amenities, and how comparatively few look around them and enjoy the wonders and delights of their new ambience.   The fact that my wife and I lived in the heart of Singapore almost automatically made us join those few, though I think and hope we would have done so anyway.   My wife has an enquiring mind, is friendly and gregarious and is fascinated by novelty.   She and I found plenty to fascinate us.

The great majority of the population of Singapore was and remains of Chinese origin.   Theirs is an old culture and civilization and not every aspect of them is readily intelligible or agreeable to Western thinking.   The comparatively transient Serviceman has especial difficulty, for the very reason of his transience.   The accepted inscrutability and mysteriousness of the Chinese are often largely in the eye of the beholder; there is much to learn and often too little time in which to learn it.   There are indeed many contradictions to be unravelled.   Acquisitiveness and avarice appear to conflict with personal generosity and hospitality; astute business sense with wild and reckless gambling; self-deprecating modesty with a very real amour-propre and sensitivity.   Above all these is ' face '.   This should never and indeed must never be lost.   Good humour rapidly disappears when it is.

For example, the Chinese driver resents being overtaken on the road, particularly by a foreigner; even more so by a woman driver; worst of all therefore by a foreign woman driver.   He will go to suicidal extremes to recover face by re-passing in such circumstances, as my wife and other Service wives found to their cost.   Not that the suicidal driving of a Singapore Chinese is readily distinguishable from his normal mode of progress.   To him a car or truck is for going, not stopping; he acknowledges the accelerator, and on occasion the clutch pedal; application of the brake loses face.   Thus such phenomena as red traffic lights and stop signs are not for him.   Red is a lucky colour anyway, and with luck the foreign devil obeying a green or go signal will stop in time.   Seat belts in Singapore are unnecessary, since the average vehicle contains such a tightly packed mass of humanity that no movement on impact or collision occurs other than a general compression.   You do not hire a taxi.   You hire a seat in one, or even a standing space if custom is brisk; and the terror and excitement of the drive dispel any thought of discomfort before the journey has scarcely started.

Legend has it that two senior Service clerics, one RAF, one Army, died at about the same time.   Both naturally ascended, and were a little put out when not immediately admitted through the pearly gates. While waiting in the ante-room for their records to be checked, they were mystified to see a small insignificant Chinese welcomed immediately on arrival, and indeed given the VIP treatment of private cloud, instant wings and fully tuned harp. The RAF padre gently accosted St Peter: ' My colleague and I, with true Christian humility, are naturally not thrusting ourselves forward, but we could not help wondering who that gentleman was who was admitted so promptly and is clearly marked for special treatment? '

' The last comer? ' replied the holy janitor. ' Let me see now—ah yes! a certain Tong Ah Wee, a Singapore taxi driver '.

' Taxi driver? But—but—may one most humbly inquire why he is given precedence over ourselves, distinguished men of orders? '

' Reverend Sirs, I can assure you that in one hour he has put the fear of God into more human souls than you two have in a lifetime of dedicated service.'

It is not only the Chinese driver who baffles and terrifies the foreigner. A pedestrian will dart briskly across in front of your car; but when you miss him by the proverbial inch, he will not swear and shake his fist. He will smile benevolently and gratefully at you. The reason is not far to seek. If he has had a hairsbreadth escape, then his personal devil—an unexplainable mixture of conscience, shadow and general private nuisance and gadfly—following as ever at his heels, has had an even more narrow escape. It has had to jump out of the way in a highly undignified manner. It has consequently lost face. And as a result it will be somewhat less of an obtrusive and persistent nuisance for the next day or two. No wonder your near-victim is grateful.

The Serviceman who takes an interest in such matters soon appreciates that the high degree of Chinese culture and civilization is nevertheless accompanied by a great variety and amount of superstition. The personal devil is only one of a whole hierarchy of such creatures that surround the Chinese in life and, worse still, in death. Due precautions must be taken in both spheres. The devotion of the Chinese to his family and ancestors is evinced very strongly in his beliefs about the hereafter. It is essential both for the well-being of the deceased and the peace of mind of those left behind that the full and exact ritual of the funeral ceremony be performed. The devils, however, always alert to discomfort and dismay, also appreciate the importance of the occasion and are on hand in great numbers and enthusiasm to produce confusion and eventual disaster. On other occasions they may be placated but here no holds are barred, the battle is à l'outrance, and no subtlety or device is missed on either side.

The first essential for the funeral conductors is to try to disguise the solemn and sorrowful nature of the occasion. With this end in view the whole affair is organized on the lines of a picnic, bean-feast or bank-holiday outing. Every friend, relative or acquaintance is mustered and hundreds of others recruited from Tongs, societies or trades unions with which the deceased may have been connected. All are issued with fireworks, gay flags, coloured hats and umbrellas, embroidered banners and bright clothing; and

93

they pile, laughing and smiling, into dozens of open lorries. With them, in a place of appropriate honour, go a large number of barrels of beer, highly ornamented and even silver plated on occasions, sometimes embowered on a lorry, sometimes proceeding on special hand-operated vehicles of their own.

The final touch is given by the brass bands. No really good funeral is complete without at least six of these, each 20 or 30 strong, and mounted on special vehicles throughout the funeral cortége. Percussion is the dominant motif. Every instrument capable of producing a loud and metallic clangour is thumped continuously and fortissimo without much regard for tempo or the tunes being played. The latter are more or less a matter of individual taste, with little conformity as between the various bands; but for some reason that I was never able to discover, ' The Flies Crawled up the Window ' has become an established and apparently perennial favourite.

The stage is thus set for the bafflement of the devils. The mourners are at their gayest and noisiest assisted by the free beer now flowing; the fireworks rattle; the band adds its cheerful din. All this row has a definite purpose. As well as being fooled by all the jollity and cheerfulness, devils are allergic to loud noises, especially in mid-afternoon (siesta time), which is consequently the chosen time for funerals. If things go according to plan they will therefore take but a cursory interest in this apparent picnic party, be distressed by the noise, and seek their diversion and their prey elsewhere; leaving the funeral to proceed according to rote and the deceased to a peaceful interment without any unwanted intruders or strange bedfellows in the grave—just himself and, of course, his inevitable personal devil.

At one stage, however, the devils, reasonably suspicious of the unnaturally large number of picnic outings that appeared to terminate somewhat unsuitably at the burial grounds, became increasingly difficult to deceive and deter, and their attendance at funerals, noise and gaiety notwithstanding, became unpleasantly pressing. However the mourners managed to remain ahead of the game. The cortége, with full complement and sound effects, still assembled behind the hearse and moved off, with the more persistent devils giving close escort; but its route to the cemetery proved strangely devious and circumambient. In the interval the deceased would be whipped out of the back door of the house, in a plain casket and into a plain van, as soon as the procession moved off; and would be duly interred and comfortably devil-proof before the spoof procession ever reached the graveside. Thus, as long as the groundwork and organization remained sound, the forces of confusion are still baffled. There should be a moral here for Service planners and administrators.

Another problem in forestalling the general devils at a funeral was of course the need to provide a full panoply of paper-made equipment to ease the deceased's sojourn in the next world. These elaborate and gaudy artifacts could scarcely escape the attention of the malevolent watchers overhead; but it was generally agreed that they could be produced and set on fire after the grave was closed and all danger had been averted. Should a heavy rainstorm threaten the burning offerings, this merely showed how angry and frustrated the devils had been at their failure; hearty laughter,

94

genuine this time, shook the mourners who had in any case forestalled this reaction by a liberal sprinkling of petrol. The elaboration and extravagance of the paper reproductions prepared for the deceased's afterlife of course varied with his status on this earth. Poor men were content with a small house, a bicycle and a reasonable amount of heavenly money; the wealthy had Cadillacs, horses, stately homes, and private aircraft—there has even been one recent report of an oil rig at a graveside.

My keen interest in such matters once nearly led me into serious trouble. While visiting Hong Kong I had been bidden to the funeral of an old Chinese friend. I did not feel inclined to take part in the false gaiety of the procession so went straight to the cemetery. On arrival I found a large crowd of mourners already gathered by the grave. As they all seemed to be concentrated on the north side, I moved round to the other side so as to get a closer farewell view. At once I was grabbed by the arm by a bystander and hurried round to join the main body. I thought at first I had committed some stupid breach of etiquette but it proved to be something much more serious. The form was this. With the deceased, a Mr Tan Baw Lee, was naturally buried his personal devil who would in duty bound accompany him to his next life. Since the necessary precautions to ward off the generality of intruding devils had been taken, everything would be in order. One Mr Tan, one personal devil duly delivered as per consignment note. But if I had persisted in standing on the south side of the grave, my own shadow (and therefore personal devil) would have been in the grave when it was filled in; and would consequently have accompanied Tan and his devil on their journey. At their destination all would have been confusion, since the books would be unbalanced by the arrival of one human soul and two devils. The Foxley-Norris devil would be an embarrassment to one and all and itself would lose intolerable face. There was only one accepted solution— send for Foxley-Norris to match the pair. I should have died within the day. It was a very narrow escape.

The Chinese of Hong Kong of course do not lag behind their fellows in Singapore when it comes to fascinating superstition. As a planner in the Far East Headquarters the RAF in Hong Kong, then quite a considerable force (who were we going to fight?), came within my sphere of responsibility, and my wife and I both became strongly attached to that enchanting place— an enchantment still real, although to some extent suffocating under the piles of concrete which now make the whole place look like a monstrous Wellsian asparagus bed. A minor crisis developed during my first visit there. The Chinese amah who served an Air Force family (our whole way of life and indeed the design of married quarters still assumed the availability of domestic servants) committed suicide by hanging after an unhappy love affair. Everyone was naturally very upset but life otherwise had to go on. It soon became apparent that this was easier said than done. The personal devils of suicides do not accompany the deceased but stay on in the place of death. Being now unattached, they promptly lose a lot of face and are consequently highly resentful and bloody minded, and become an infernal nuisance to all concerned. No Chinese in her right mind would enter service in such a house, nor would tradesmen or paper-boys even call. Eventually the married quarter had to be vacated and stood empty and unrented. This naturally generated indignant comment from the Air Ministry financiers, but at the end of the day they had to foot the bill for an exorcist, who conducted a prolonged and costly spiritual fumigation of the house, insisting incidentally on total redecoration (including much red paint) and replacement of all carpets, curtains and furnishings. This did the trick and there was no further trouble for future tenants; but what the auditors made of this substantial budget item we were never privileged to know.

An even more dramatic incident occurred later, when it was decided to instal a large modern radar station on the top of a precipitous peak in Hong Kong's New Territories. This hill-top was called Tai Mo Shan and an access to it had to be constructed by carving a roadway out of the cliff face. Road-making machines could not undertake this task and it had to be manually performed by coolie labour, much of which incidentally was provided by the unique order of red-scarved celibate women workers who are to be found all over the Far East. Construction proved difficult, prolonged and hazardous, two of the unfortunate coolies falling to their deaths in the process. Finally, however, the road emerged on to the gently sloping plateau on the top of which the radar station was to be erected. At this stage all the workers suddenly downed tools and flatly refused to extend the roadway a yard further.

The British supervisors were confounded and totally baffled. Why stop now? The difficult and dangerous bit lay behind them. Why not finish the job in a matter of days and go home rejoicing?

Higher wages and other inducements were offered but the workers stood firm in their refusal. After prolonged negotiations the cause of the trouble emerged. Apparently it was well known that there was a powerful and dangerous dragon asleep just under the surface at the very top of the hill where the radars were to be located. He had been dormant and harmless for many years now; but naturally the sound of digging and levelling would disturb him. Roused, probably somewhat ill-tempered, from his long slumbers, he would immediately observe this splendid new highway reaching right to his door and apparently built for his benefit; giving, as it would, ready access to the fertile and heavily populated valleys below. He would lose no time in descending and spreading fire, pestilence and general mayhem among the entire community. The road-workers were certainly not going to be responsible for letting loose something so lethal on that community, including as it did their own families.

There was total deadlock, in spite of eloquent pleading and mounting offers of bribes. While the impasse held, a million pounds worth of radar and communications equipment lay useless in its crates at the foot of the mountain. At last someone had the bright idea of sending for Mr Davenport. Who might he be? He was, it appeared, an Englishman who had spent his whole life in the colony and spent much of that life studying Chinese beliefs and traditions, on which he had become an acknowledged authority.

He arrived, a distinguished white-haired gentleman, leaning heavily on a

Above: 'The eyes (and unfortunately the ears) of Texas are on us.'   Cadet Tour, USA, 1949.   [USAF

Below: Oxford University Air Squadron at home, 1949.   [Crown Copyright

Above: 'Ugh, what have I done?'
Post-aerobatics, OUAS, 1949.
[Crown Copyright

Right: Author/Comedy Lead with
straight man; Staff College Pantomime,
1951. *[Crown Copyright*

Left: 'You know your trouble? Your shorts are too short.' Singapore, 1955.

Below: 'And how was your trip, Miss Sheridan?' JLF-N as hostess, 1955.

Above left: 'Oh Genevieve, sweet Genevieve.'   Kenneth More, West Malling, 1956.

Left: 'The dinner that nearly dished me.'   HQ Fighter Command, 1958.   *[Air Ministry*

Above: Hunter as Woodburner; Stradishall, 1959.   *[Crown Copyright*

Left: 'This is your life, and mine too as it turned out.' Leonard Cheshire, 1960. *[BBC*

Below left: 'It seems there were these two Irishmen...' Assistant Chief of Defence Staff, 1964. *[Crown Copyright*

Right: 'One of your damned police dogs must have got it.' AOC 224 Group, Singapore, 1964. *[Crown Copyright*

Below: 'Parade ready for inspection, Sir.' Royal Australian Air Force, Butterworth, 1965. *[Crown Copyright*

Above: Far East helicopters.
Belvederes over Singapore, 1965.
[Crown Copyright

Left: And their usual operational
conditions.   Borneo during
'Confrontations'.   *[Crown Copyright*

Right: 60 Squadron RAF 50th
Anniversary, Singapore, 1966.
[Crown Copyright

Above left: 'Down wind is easy.'
Singapore, 1966.

Above: The shape of things to come.
JLF-N with handicapped children,
Singapore, 1966.

Left: 'Shouldn't it look at me and not the
camera?' Arrival of the C-in-C,
Germany, 1968.

Above right: 'On the way up.'
Chancellor Schmidt as Minister of
Defence visits HQ Germany, 1968.

Right: General Johannes Steinhoff,
Inspector General of the Luftwaffe, and
friends, 1969.

Right: 'For crissakes mind where you put that goddam foot!' Phantom F-4, 1969.

Below: 'Hope you'll find our product satisfactory, Sir.' Group Captain John Cunningham, 1970.

HAWKER SIDDELEY HARRIER

Left: 'Funny, it seemed to me we were flying backwards!'   Harrier, 1970.

Below: 'It's bound to come down sometime.'   RAF Ancients v Army Antiquities, 1969.

Above left: 'There you are, we knew he'd overdo the bonhomie.'   Visit of HRH Princess Anne, 1970.

Left: 'Ven the Prince jokes, you laugh Bertie.'   Visit of HRH Prince Bernhard and General Wolf, Netherlands Air Force, 1970.

Above: 'What tune are they trying to sing dear?'

Right: 'That old black magic.'   Farewell to Germany, November 1970.

Above: 'Are you under there lad?'   CPL inspects Winchester College CCF, 1973.
[*E. A. Sollers*

Below left: 'When is a haggis not a haggis?   Go on, tell me.'   Visit of CPL to Hong Kong, 1973.

Below right: 'Yes, yes, but what happens when he closes it?'   Visit of HRH The Prince of Wales to CFS Little Rissington, 1973.

stick. The matter was explained to him. He had a quiet word with the foreman of the coolies. A solution was soon agreed. All that was needed was the erection across the road of an old fashioned European-type customs barrier, two knife-rest supports carrying a wooden pole which could be raised or lowered. When it had been provided, Mr Davenport undertook to have the pole painted with dragon-proof paint (which turned out to be a sort of mottled green colour). If this were done, and a promise given that the pole would always be in the down position except during the passage of a vehicle, the work could be resumed and the road completed.

And it was so. The radars were duly installed and functioned well, without dragon interference. And I am told that to this day the barrier procedure is carefully observed. Dragons are known to sleep with one eye open.

I should not like to give the impression that the Chinese is exclusively preoccupied with consideration of the afterworld and its denizens. While spared in this life, he enjoys the good things of it—including a multiplicity of wives, if they can be placed in this category. These have a strict and rigidly observed pecking order, Number One being very much the boss lady whatever the attractions of her juniors; and numbers five and six downwards being far less cabined and confined. Socially the Chinese is a charming and generous host, whose standard of hospitality is high and unvarying—often dangerously so. He is a hard drinker who, like the Russian, drinks his toasts standing, downing them neat and at one gulp; his guests, to avoid offence, must follow suit. This ceremony is preceded by cries of ' Yam Seng ' (bottoms up) becoming louder, more frequent and more staccato as the evening progresses. Unfortunately for the guests, custom permits the host two advantages. Firstly he can, and often does, give his servants prior briefing that every third or even second drink poured into his own brandy glass (brandy is much favoured during as well as after meals) should in fact be cold tea, a privilege not extended to the guests. Secondly, local etiquette finds nothing unusual in the host at a later stage being raised and lowered from his chair for Yam Sengs by a couple of servants. Here again the guest, depending on natural resources, is facing heavy odds.

Local drinking habits have few subtleties; a bottle of whisky or brandy often flanks each plate, failure to empty which unforgiveably costs one's host's face. Most of the traditional dishes are now internationally known, the shark's fin soup, the sea-slug and the hundred-year old egg. Incidentally the age of the latter is much exaggerated; an egg is considered of quite reasonable vintage, and palatable to all except the strictest gourmet, at any age over five years. Dinners frequently comprise up to 14 courses and unfortunately, particularly in open-air restaurants, neither their number nor order is predictable. The dishes, of astonishing volume and variety, are served as each happens to reach the correct stage of preparation. It is thus almost impossible to adjust one's consumption to appetite in order to last the full meal, which is de rigueur.

The duration of parties at certain times of the year is just as unpredictable. These are the moon-flower parties. A particularly beautiful species, something akin to a water-lily, the moon-flower blooms and dies in one night; and the party coincides with it. The guests assemble; the flower opens; the eating and drinking get under way; finally the flower suddenly withers and droops; the guests follow suit. The trick for foreigners to watch for here is a tendency for the thirsty number one son to substitute surreptitiously a more recent and fresher bloom when the original one shows signs of imminent decease.

The chopstick is the universal eating implement, and takes rather less mastering than might be imagined. The secret, as in golf, is to keep the head well down. The closer the proximity between mouth and eating bowl, the greater the intake and the less the spillage. Chinese gentlemen of the old school can transfer a bowlful of nourishment to the mouth in under two minutes, and the whole spectacle has something of the dignified efficiency and persistence of a Thames dredger in high gear. Conversation meanwhile is at a discount but certain social conventions replace it. Choice morsels, such as a fish's eyeball, may be selected and fed courteously to one's neighbour. There are traps for the unwary here, however, as my wife found in our early days. The acceptance of three such titbits from the same gentleman at one sitting amounts to a tacit agreement by the lady to the status of concubinage. There is considered to be nothing immoral or disgraceful about this position, which is indeed much sought after and sparingly bestowed; nevertheless its acceptance, especially at the outset of a tour of duty abroad, could have led to obvious complications. I am glad to say that these were evaded without offence being given, or face (or indeed anything else) lost.

Since it suited both the authorities and myself, my tour of duty in Singapore had been extended to more than three years. Two to two and a half was the accepted maximum, since thereafter the monotonous climate, unvaryingly hot and humid (it has been said that in Singapore in the dry season, it rains every day; in the wet season it rains all day), tends to make one bad-tempered and dull-witted. Perhaps it did; or perhaps I was spared because my constant professional travels through such widely separated areas as Korea, Washington, Britain and Australasia saved me the full monotony. Be that as it may, it was with genuine regret that I saw the end of my tour approach and finally arrive.

We had both of us found a new and strange environment, but one in which we would never feel strangers again. We had high hopes that this would not be the last time we should live in it; nor was it. Our stay terminated on a typically bizarre note.

In preparation for our return home by troopship (which incidentally was the last through Suez before the war started) we invited a firm of Chinese removal men to come and pack up our worldly goods for the journey; we had acquired quite a large hoard of these during a stay of more than three years but we had no qualms about their safety since the Chinese are the most meticulous packers in the world. Each breakable item is swaddled in shredded paper, then in a cocoon of straw and finally in a tube of corrugated cardboard. Our only concern—I have mentioned that we had established a routine of renting luxurious mansions from businessmen on leave—was to ensure that there was no confusion between our own chattels and those of our hosts.   I solved this problem by clearing the large drawing room of all our landlord's furniture and possessions, and putting all our own into that one room.   The movers were instructed to pack everything in that room and nothing else (the furniture would be replaced after we had left).   A simple and indeed masterly plan.

When we arrived back in England and started to unpack I had one packing case for which I could not account.   It contained thirty nine cardboard tubes; each one proved to contain an electric light bulb (there had been a large chandelier in that drawing room).   Chinese packers are, as I said, meticulous.   An apologetic cable and a cheque closed that chapter.

14 Fighter Command Revisited

On my return home I had twin ambitions, to resume full flying duties and, if possible, to be promoted; I had by then (the late summer of 1956) been a Wing Commander on and off for twelve years, substantively for more than five. I made these proposals at interview with the Air Secretary's staff. At the idea of making me a Group Captain they fell about laughing; but when they had pulled themselves together, they agreed to give me a good flying appointment. I was to become Wing Commander Flying at West Malling; this was a famous night fighter station in Kent, so I was well pleased. But first I had to be initiated into the art of night-fighting and I went off to the conversion unit at North Luffenham, where I set up some sort of a local record by doing more than a hundred hours flying in the Meteor aircraft in less than two months. I also recorded a ' Mayday ' SOS call when on one dark night I found myself at maximum altitude over the middle of the North Sea with insufficient fuel to get home owing to freezing in the pipe lines between the overload and main tanks. Fortunately for my navigator and myself they thawed out on the way down.

The Meteor NF 12/14 was a good solid aircraft, a steady gun-platform and pleasant to fly, although the overload tanks we had to carry to give adequate endurance markedly impaired its manoeuvrability. The fact remained, however, that it was not up to the job; and the crews knew it. It just did not have the performance to intercept or overhaul the latest Russian bombers, against which it was designed to defend the country by night or in foul weather. There is nothing worse for the morale of aircrew, or for that matter any member of any Service, than to know that his equipment will not serve its purpose or match that of the enemy when put to the ultimate test. After all, the final objective of all military training is, or should be, to develop combat capability. When men, from high commanders down to the ' workers at the coal face ', know that such combat capability cannot be attained with the weapons given to them, training becomes a ritual pavane, an artificial exercise from which all spirit is lost since no credibility exists. It is too little appreciated that this is not only bad for morale but also for recruiting. If armed forces are manned, as ours are, on an all-volunteer basis, those volunteers will not be forthcoming if it is obvious that in the event they can serve no realistic purpose.

Having completed my own specialist training, I returned to West Malling and settled down for what promised to be a worthwhile and enjoyable two or three years. West Malling had four jet fighter squadrons, one of which I was delighted to find came from my old love the Royal Auxiliary Air Force (No 501 County of Kent Squadron). At this stage of the game, however, the Air Secretary played his joker. Having ridiculed the very idea a mere three months before, he now told me I was to be promoted acting Group Captain and become the Chief of Plans at Headquarters Fighter Command. Rather desperately my wife started to reload our scarcely unloaded packing-cases for the move to Stanmore.

The appointment proved to be demanding and interesting although not always exactly in the manner I had envisaged. I recall that after taking over, my ' first solo ' was to participate in a day-long conference on the comparative merits for our air defence system of the analogue and digital computers. As I had at that stage no idea what either term meant, I was able to contribute little of value to the debate. However, one soon learned what it was all about; and here, as always, I was admirably supported by a loyal efficient staff, led at that time by my old friend Dennis Crowley-Milling.

In 1956 Fighter Command was still a very big organization with more than 40 squadrons (including the Auxiliaries) located on half as many airfields, together with a large number of associated subordinate Head-quarters, early warning and ground control radar stations with elaborate alert communications, surface to air missile sites and training and support units of various types. The Command Headquarters itself was proportion-ately large and active to match its responsibility for the defence of the country against conventional or nuclear bombers, both of which were still regarded as presenting a serious threat to the national security. We were of course also an integral part of the NATO air defence system, which involved considerable international liaison and co-operation. The Commander in Chief was Air Marshal Sir Thomas Pike. He had established a well-earned reputation as one of the most effective night-fighter pilots of the earlier days of the war. He was a quiet spoken, serious minded, somewhat shy and reticent man, who did not fit the accepted image of the dashing fighter leader; but he had much strength of character and was a man of great integrity and high moral principles, and at the same time real understanding and humanity. In conversation he was not amusing or easily amused, but he perceived the essential aspects of any problem and ensured that they were never over-looked. I learned a great deal at his feet and know that I owed much of any later success I achieved to his influence and example.

On one occasion an important policy conference convened under his chairmanship. Its subject was the introduction of the new runway barriers on all fighter airfields. These, bearing some resemblance to high aluminium-corded tennis nets, were designed to catch and slow aircraft overshooting the runway on landing, through brake failure, icing or aquaplaning, or mere error of judgment. Such a mishap with high speed aircraft in the past usually destroyed the aeroplane and often killed or seriously injured the crew. The barriers were intended to absorb the initial shock and momentum of the aircraft's impact, keep it on its wheels and reduce damage to both airframe and crew. They eventually proved a godsend; but at that stage there was still much controversy about their design, materials, method of operation and indeed actual justification.

The argument finally boiled down to one major issue. Should the barrier

101

be permanently installed in the fully upright position? Or should it have a snap-up-and-down facility, operated from the air traffic control tower? The former solution involved serious operational hazards because of the real risk of accidental engagement by aircraft taking off or landing over such an obstruction; the latter, with all its extra cables and communications, would be much more expensive. Those present aligned themselves accordingly, the pilots on the staff insisting that the dangers of the fixed installation were too high; the financiers objecting to the expense of the more flexible system.

Sir Thomas, as an operational pilot of much experience, came down firmly in favour of the snap-up version.

' It is quite apparent to me ', he pronounced, ' that permanent erection is not only undesirable but unacceptable '.

Nobody disagreed—and nobody laughed.

I recall another moment of drama and perhaps humour. In 1956 the Command was about to be re-equipped with the English Electric Lightning fighter, whose performance was incomparably better than that of any of our previous aircraft. Unfortunately, having a much higher wing-loading, it also had to make its approach and landing much faster; and consequently required a much longer and stronger runway than had sufficed for our Meteors and Hunters. Nearly every Fighter Command runway would have to be rebuilt and nearly every airfield consequently have to be closed for a long period (involving the temporary relocation of most of our squadrons), not just those re-equipping with the Lightning, since for operational flexibility and bad weather diversion the latter had to be able to use almost any runway in the Command. Throughout the exercise, lasting a good three years, the Command must be able to maintain a full number of squadrons at operational readiness in case of emergency.

The job of working out this complicated process, a sort of combination of snakes and ladders, three dimensional noughts and crosses and time and motion study, naturally fell to the planners. After much discussion and writing of studies, we produced our master plan. This was recognized to be such a major project, so costly to the Air Force Vote and of such general interest, that the Commander in Chief invited some members of the Air Council to attend the presentation of our proposals. I viewed the attendant high-ranking audience with some natural apprehension but we had great faith in the merits of our plan. The modus operandi was to be that I would speak for about threequarters of an hour. Behind me was an immense chart illustrating all the proposed construction schedules and the consequent moves of squadrons. The whole was divided into three-monthly sections and covered with a series of blanking paper strips. As I came to discuss each quarterly period, Dennis Crowley-Milling would pull off the relevant strip and disclose our suggested solution.

I commenced by explaining that the whole plan was essentially based on the heavy use by our older aircraft of a few airfields whose runways, often for topographical reasons, could not be extended (West Malling, on top of its Kentish hill, was one such). These I would refer to as ' bolt-holes ' and I stressed their critical contribution to the plan, accepting some short term unavoidable but operationally undesirable overcrowding. After five or ten minutes I was well into my stride and gaining confidence all the while, when from the back row rose the familiar figure of Mr Bill Cousins, the Command Engineer, responsible under the Air Ministry Works Department for all our building and construction.

' Christopher ', he said, ' I know I shouldn't interrupt at this stage but it already looks to me as if your plan depends heavily on RAF Stradishall as one of your essential bolt-hole airfields '.

' That's right, Bill ', I replied. ' We aim to operate it to maximum capacity during the whole reconstruction period '.

' Well, that's very unfortunate ', he answered. ' I think someone on my staff should have told you that the runway there is subsiding seriously owing to bad drainage. There's an urgent need to relay it and it will be out of action for at least a year. Inevitable, I'm afraid '.

There ensued what is generally referred to as a pregnant pause. After reflection I turned to Sir Thomas.

' Sir, I think we shall have to tear up the whole plan and start again.'

After an even longer pause, he gave his ruling, concise and decisive as always. ' Yes, I'm afraid you will. Do that, please.'

And so we did. The distinguished audience adjourned somewhat prematurely to the bar; and the planners retired to their offices and called for black coffee.

Most RAF officers, apart from their primary responsibilities, undertake what are referred to as secondary duties. In late 1957 I was invited by the Commander in Chief to do a spell as President of the Mess Committee at the Headquarters. This job was never a sinecure, since, although there was a large and competent full-time staff to run the domestic affairs of the Mess, there was still a great deal of supervision and co-ordination to be done and a considerable work-load of protocol, mess functions, ceremonial visits and so on. My own term of office (by design, I was kindly told) was to include a unique occasion of this nature. On 1 April 1958 the Royal Air Force would celebrate its fortieth anniversary and the main feature of the celebrations would be a full scale ceremonial dinner at the Fighter Command Mess at Bentley Priory. The entire adult Royal Family were invited to attend and had graciously accepted.

The PMC would have a lot of work to do and carry a heavy responsibility. I had a nasty foreboding that this was one of those all too common occasions when, if everything goes well, everyone involved indulges in a great deal of gratuitous self-congratulation; if anything goes seriously wrong, a head must roll—and the shoulders on which it sat would not be far to seek. I felt some sense of resentment about this. I had joined the air force to fly; and later, as it turned out, to command and to serve on the professional staff. If I had made a through nonsense of any of these three activities, I should have had only myself to blame for any consequent penalties. But I had not joined to serve as a sort of glorified maitre d'hotel, and, as the eunuch said in the story, I was perhaps not cut out for the job; yet, if anything were to go seriously wrong on the big night, my name would inevitably and enduringly be mud. I would figure in everybody's recollection as ' that chap who made such a hash of the Royal Dinner'. It was not an altogether cheerful prospect.

The preparatory phases had some awkward and some amusing moments. The main dining room at Bentley Priory is an unlovely single-storey extension of the original eighteenth century building, of peculiar shape in that it is basically rectangular but has a sort of extruded salient at one corner. It is small in capacity, seating only about one hundred diners. Hence many noses would have to be put out of joint by the need for strict rationing of invitations, especially since the great men of the RAF's past as well as its present must be there, in addition to some inevitable politicians and civil servants. Additionally there were complications such as TV cameramen, newsreel and press photographers, commentators, reporters and so on. I decided that it would not be practicable, or enjoyable for the distinguished company to have all these people in the actual room. We thought up the idea of building externally a sort of raised hide, on the outside of the extruded corner of the dining room to accommodate the men from the media and their paraphernalia. It would look rather peculiar from the driveway and I was not sure that the Royal party and other VVIP diners would appreciate the many-eyed Argus of lenses peering down at them from the far end of the hall. But I imagined they would be pretty well accustomed to it; and in any case I could think of no alternative solution.

The members of the Air Council, including the CAS himself, Sir Dermot Boyle, took an active and personal interest in the preparations for the affair, on which the good name of the Royal Air Force as a host would much depend and which would be exposed to so much publicity. Visiting in late February and taking luncheon in the Mess, Sir Dermot enquired of me: ' Where are you going to put the band, Foxley?'

' Band, Sir? Nobody's said anything about a band.'

' Good Lord, man, use your head. Of course we've got to have a band. We must have the traditional RAF music, the Lincolnshire Poacher, the Post Horn Gallop and all that.'

' Yes, Sir, I suppose so. But where are we going to put the band?'

' Don't ask *me*—why don't you put them in that corner place over there?'

I explained about the hide for the cameras intruding somewhat into that space already.

' Well, in that case the band will just have to sit in a single row under that hide of yours.'

So it was settled. I must confess that I was a little concerned about what Her Majesty would make of this rather odd spectacle of a single rank small orchestra, surmounted by a battery of cameras; but again there seemed no alternative.

At our next meeting a week or so later, the CAS bowled me another bumper. ' Who've we got to paint the picture, Foxley?'

' Picture, Sir? Nobody's said anything about a picture.' (This was getting monotonous.)

' Of course we must have a picture. We must have a really fine painting

104

of such a splendid historic occasion; every officers' mess will want a copy.'

' Yes, Sir. But where are we going to put the artist?'

' Don't ask *me*—put him in the band.'

And it was so. Her Majesty was going to observe an even more unusual arrangement. In the event it proved even more unusual than anyone anticipated. A famous artist of proven skill was selected to paint the required picture (a copy of which does indeed now hang in every RAF Officers' Mess). It so happened that he was deaf and dumb and had to be accompanied on such occasions by his tall and handsome wife, who interpreted for him in manual sign language. So that the Queen was finally faced with was a battery of cameras poking aggressively apparently through the outside wall of the building; an orchestra bizarrely arranged in Indian file; an artist busy at his easel; and an inexplicable lady in full evening dress standing at his side and gesticulating rapidly. I often wonder what Her Majesty made of it.

If the rehearsal for the event was full of such incident, it was as nothing to the actual performance. One or two details stand out vividly in my mind—or in recurrent nightmares.

The Queen's retiring room was arranged in a small ante room, known as Queen Adelaide's Room since history related that that unhappy lady died there. Normally in use by a personal assistant, it was for this occasion to be specially fitted out by a famous furniture-hire firm; an easy chair; a long mirror, a rug; a dressing table and a sitting stool to be placed in front of it. The latter had what I as a layman would call ' wrap-over ' legs, passing from under each corner of the seat to the opposite corner at floor level. A senior WRAF officer was busy checking these arrangements and making minor adjustments as women will. She was about to move the stool slightly when a cleaning lady, also busy in the room, called across sharply to her: ' I wouldn't touch that, Ma'am '.

' Oh, why not?'

' Well it collapses—it's busted you see.'

And she proceeded to demonstrate the truth of her statement by gentle pressure of her hand. It duly collapsed. We supposed that the previous hirers of the stool had managed to break it, and not wishing to pay the costs had just jammed the splintered legs together without repair or adhesive. But for that admirable cleaning lady—the mind boggles.

But this was as nothing to a later moment of almost unbearable drama. To relate this story, I must perforce give some explanation of the layout of Bentley Priory and the protocol arrangements for the ceremony.

Guests enter the building through a lofty mirrored hallway with, in terms of a stage set, a flight of stairs ascending front left; and tall double doors giving access near left to the ' Rotunda '. This Rotunda is a handsome circular reception room, glass-domed right to the roof and hung with portraits of fighter aces of the past. Rear right is a suite of cloakroom and toilet facilities; front right a long passage leads to the dining room already described.

The ceremonial was to proceed as follows. VIP guests would arrive by

1915 hours and be entertained in a large ante-room at the rear of the building, taking their places at dinner before 2000 hours. After 1915 VVIP guests would begin to arrive precisely spaced at two minute intervals, use the cloak-rooms if required, and then pass into the Rotunda for refreshment; each was to be provided with a personal escorting officer to shepherd him through this process. The Queen's arrival was timed for 2000 hours; she was to travel from Windsor by car, a distance of perhaps twenty miles.

The same time was chosen for the start of the TV programme. The first 10 minutes of this were to be taken up by a commentary by that past-master of such affairs, Richard Dimbleby; he would indicate and describe all the historic mementos on display, the silver, the trophies, the pictures and the Standards assembled in the dining room. I was stationed in the centre rear of the entrance hallway. Richard and I had no walkie-talkie but we had evolved a system of push-bell signals for communication; one buzz was an affirmative; two a negative. At ten minutes past eight he was to signal the finish of his conducted tour of the dining-room. I would acknowledge and, if all was well, the action would be switched to the cameras in the hallway; and a minute or two later I would open the Rotunda double doors for the Royal and VVIP cortege to process under the camera's eye to the dining room.

It all sounded very straightforward and had proved so at the dress rehearsal two nights previously. Initially once again matters went smoothly. The VVIP guests arrived, each to the appointed minute, were offered the cloak-room and conducted to the Rotunda. One male guest declined the offer, saying that he preferred to accept it at the last minute ' after Her Majesty arrives '. There would be time enough; he proceeded to the Rotunda and was duly refreshed.

At 2000 hours the TV cameras in the dining room whirred into action and Dimbleby followed suit. At 2010 hours he gave the PMC the agreed signal; he had finished, and the scene should switch accordingly to the hallway and the Rotunda doors. The unhappy PMC had to reply with a firmly negative double buzz. Her Majesty had not yet arrived. Normally world-famous for her precise punctuality, her car had become inextricably jammed behind a multiple road-accident en route through the suburbs, and even her police escort could not find her a quick way through.

The imperturbable Dimbleby recommenced his saga—incidentally catching the unhappy officer guarding the Royal Standard, who naturally thought that bit was all over, in an enormous yawn. At 2012 hours Her Majesty arrived, all apologies, and was duly conducted to the Rotunda to complete the party. The PMC, much relieved, transmitted the signal allowing the camera cover to be switched to its double doors.

At that moment the self-same doors swung open abruptly, and the above-mentioned VVIP re-emerged smartly through them, his escort officer flapping around him like an anxious hen, and enquiring loudly as he came: ' Now—where can I get a pee? Where can I get a pee? '

Five seconds later he would inexorably and explicitly have filled the TV screens of the nation. The swooning PMC transmitted a frenzied and unintelligible hurricane of buzzes to Dimbleby in the dining room. And that gallant warrior, to the total mystification of among others all our wives who were watching the scene on the TV at the Commander in Chief's house and, who having played in the rehearsal, knew that something was sadly amiss, once again took up his thrice-told tale.

By 2015 the VVIP was restored to his place. For the last time I transferred the TV coverage; and respectfully opened those double doors through which the royal cortege graciously processed to its dinner.

My wife tells me that my hair greyed by several shades during those weeks. This proved to be a blessing in disguise. Until then, at 40 years of age I still held the substantive rank of Wing Commander, albeit Acting Group Captain. Being of somewhat youthful appearance still, the word around the clubs was that young Foxley was doing quite well, having made Wing Commander. After April 1958, the tune began to change. ' Don't tell me ', they whispered, ' that old Foxley is *still* a Wing Commander? ' In consequence (I presumed), I was in fact promoted three times in the next six years. It was perhaps not an altogether ill-wind that had blown through those Rotunda doors.

Taking pity on my now obviously galloping senesence and imminent nervous breakdown, Sir Thomas Pike fulfilled a promise he had made two years before when I was snatched untimely from my flying appointment. My time as a planner was confined to a bare two years; and after a conversion course onto the Javelin night fighter I went happily off to Suffolk to command RAF Stradishall, now duly fitted with its nice new runway that had given me such a headache once before.

15 How he does go on, doesn't he

Just as the happiest days of most men are supposed to be their school days, the best years for a serving officer are reputedly those spent in command. Whether this is always so I take leave to doubt since there must always be variations of taste (I have even been asked to accept that some people are actually happy in Whitehall); but for me it was certainly true, and my wife shared my opinion as she shared our happiness.

Stradishall offered some indisputable attractions. I took over from a highly efficient officer who had not been too well liked; this incidentally is something everyone should aim to do since you are made very welcome, yet do not have to overwork cleaning up your predecessor's mistakes. The station had three resident fighter squadrons, two equipped with the twin-engined Javelin night fighter and one with the single engined day fighter/ground attack Hunter. The latter was a joy to fly; the former was not. A great heavy brute of a machine, its aerodynamic qualities were such that it was nicknamed the Dragmaster. However, unlike the Meteor, it was at least designed for the job and might have been able to perform it efficiently had it been able to exceed the speed of sound. Additionally, because of the aforementioned general runway extension programme, we frequently had other squadrons temporarily attached. So the station was full of men and aircraft, and both were kept busy.

Stradishall is in north-west Suffolk, a lovely piece of country with most hospitable and friendly natives. By now there are certain parts of Britain where the presence of the Royal Air Force has become an accepted and indeed welcome part of the way of life. East Anglia is one, just as other areas offer traditional homes for the Navy and the Army. Although the increasing noise of aircraft disturbed and annoyed people, and the behaviour of young officers and airmen off-duty occasionally did the same, on the whole we were treated very much as part of the family. We shared and enjoyed all the pursuits and activities of the local society (in its original sense); and it was perhaps only later when one moved to less friendly and receptive surroundings that one appreciated one's good fortune.

Apart from the brief spell at West Malling in 1956, it was the first time in 13 years that I had lived on an operational station and been closely associated with its people and activities. This may sound surprising but was not all that unusual at that time. Furthermore my last comparable experience had been in wartime, so I expected to have to learn a lot. On the surface perhaps much had changed, but, fundamentally, very little. The basic activity, preparing and flying aircraft operationally, had altered only insofar as aircraft performance, scientific advances and specialized techniques had developed. The men themselves had on the whole the same qualities, interests and activities. It was a pleasant surprise to find how easy and enjoyable it was to slip back into the way of life.

One noticeable change was in the breed of officers. They were for the most part not of the traditional officer class, that is to say public-school educated sons of gentlemen. The reason for this was not far to seek. The performance of their aircraft and the professional skills required meant that they had to be very special people, very carefully selected. Strength of character and quickness of intelligence were essential; it takes a brave and clever man to get the most out of a modern fighter aircraft. Ideally, of course, the officer should also have high social attributes; but if these are not inherent, they can be instilled, whereas brains and bravery cannot. I was silly enough to let this lack of traditional qualities worry me at one stage; but an older and wiser man, with major responsibility for the selection of officers, put me right: ' Look, this is how it goes. Like it or not, what we are offered nowadays as a general rule—of course, there are plenty of exceptions—is the first eleven from Nerdleigh Grammar School or the third eleven from Eton and Harrow. Frankly, the latter just don't measure up to the job. The former do, and, given a little polishing up, are just as good in some ways and a damn sight better where it counts '.

He was right. The most promising young officer on the strength at Stradishall was the son of a coal-face miner; and there were many like him.

The natural talents of these young men were such that, with appropriate training and supervision, the graph of their personal potential soon began to rise rapidly, offering limitless prospects. There remained one problem. In line with the current trend, they mostly married early; and, to use a piece of deplorable old-fashioned snobbery, they sometimes married beneath them. By this I mean that, whereas for the men any social deficiencies were far outweighed by assets of character and personality, the same only too often did not apply to the girls they chose to marry. It was depressing to have to observe time and again that same graph for a young officer rising steeply from a low base-line, only to be brought down to a nadir again by a premature unsuitable marriage, early multiple parenthood and all the social difficulties and financial problems (as usual in peacetime we were grossly underpaid and the obsolete rule by which there were no marriage allowances below a given age still applied) from which he rarely succeeded in recovering.

The regulation under which an officer had to obtain his Commanding Officer's permission to marry had, probably rightly, been abolished. However, he still had to give his CO due notice of his intention to wed; and here I saw the makings of a solution. To my somewhat cynical mind, the young virile officer was in many cases basically seeking an outlet for his virility. If the lady concerned was unwilling to act as such without the reassurance of a wedding ring—which, believe it or not, was known to happen in those days, at least in Suffolk—more was the pity, but so be it. It occurred to me that we might learn from our French and German allies, and establish an official brothel. Then when Flying Officer Smith reported to me on a given Tuesday that he was contemplating marriage, and if I in my self-appointed wisdom thought it likely to prove unfortunate for him, I would say mere, 'Smith, you are attached to the Station brothel for a period of 48 hours. Come and see me again on Friday'.

I had good grounds for believing that in many cases Friday's interview would produce an admission that that indeed was what he had had in mind; and could his application to marry be withdrawn? Where indeed true love inspired the latter, all would proceed as planned and no harm done—perhaps indeed some valuable experience gained. I therefore indented to Headquarters Fighter Command for a station brothel for RAF Stradishall; and sat back to await results.

These were not long in coming. I received a telephone call from Air Vice Marshal Eric Butler, the Air Officer in Charge of Administration, a good friend and a man of humour and humanity.

'Christopher? I shall be in your part of the world next weekend. I'd like to drop by on my journey home and spend Monday with you. Some time since I've been to Stradishall, I'm afraid; I'd like to see how you're all getting on.'

'Next Monday, Sir? Yes, that would be fine—we've only got a routine exercise on. Shall we look forward to seeing you about mid-morning?'

'Splendid, about ten-thirty then. No ceremonial, please, just ordinary working routine.'

At 1030 precisely the 2-starred car drew up outside my office. The Air Vice Marshal was on benign form as usual, though perhaps abnormally probing in his questions to officers and men. However, all went very well. The operational flying was on schedule; performance and morale could be seen to be good; and everyone gave a fully justified impression of efficiency and cheerfulness. We enjoyed a companionable lunch in the Mess and adjourned once more to my office for discussions. Eric Butler came straight to the point.

'Look, I don't pretend to know what's going on—everything seems perfectly normal here, no unusual problems or worries, in fact all highly satisfactory. Just what the devil are you up to this time?'

I explained the thinking behind my proposal. After he had stopped laughing, he said he quite agreed but the request was formally and finally rejected—and would I stop spreading alarm and despondency in his HQ? He went on his way, somewhat relieved, I suspect. I understood that inter alia Lady Astor would not have liked the idea of my brothel; though quite how she would have been involved was not entirely clear to me.

In spite of this particular disappointment, I remained most impressed by the professional performance and high spirit of my people. That spirit could well have been lowered by various factors. Our subsonic aircraft were not really up to the job and the men knew it. Furthermore the short flight endurance of the Hunter in particular in the unpredictable weather of East Anglia lent real hazards to operational exercises. One of my dashing young men, caught out in widespread and unexpected fog, scraped into a neighbouring bomber airfield with empty tanks but with most of a large apple tree projecting from his starboard intake. As a woodburner, however,

110

the Hunter proved disappointing and the experiment was carried no further.

Nor was morale much to be encouraged by the antics of higher defence authority. The Lord had apparently appeared in a dream to the then Secretary of State for Defence, Mr Duncan Sandys (for there could be no other logical explanation for his policies), and tipped him off that all future warfare would be largely conducted by the use of missiles, with a consequent reduction in the requirement for such things as manned aircraft inter alia. When this revelation was made public to a reverent world, the Daily Express carried an inch-high headline ' FIGHTER COMMAND—THE END '; and generally speaking there would have been some justification for a degree of at least uncertainty, if not actual pessimism. That neither materialized said much for the character and good sense of those on the receiving end.

So life at Stradishall was very good. It was therefore quite a shock when in the autumn of 1959 I was told I was to remove to West Malling, shortly to re-open after extensive repolishment. Although Malling was for us an old and happy home, I naturally queried the reason for such an early change of station. I was informed, in strict confidence, that the days of Stradishall were numbered; it was to close as a flying station, and I should think myself very lucky to command a second fighter base. I therefore held my peace and until now have continued to do so, even though, in the event, West Malling closed within a year of our arrival there whereas Stradishall enjoyed a further dozen years of happy and active life. Ah well! you can't win them all, as we planners say.

West Malling again proved a most challenging and enjoyable command. The enjoyment came as usual from the work, the company and the country-side. The challenge came from the denizens of the latter. Not here the long-established friendship and partnership of East Anglia. The natives of Kent apparently had shorter memories, perhaps because many of those concerned were not in fact natives but immigrant stock brokers, insurance-men and other commuters. They had come to Kent for peace and quiet, either at weekends or for future retirement. The arrival of two squadrons of Javelins, admittedly a deplorably noisy aircraft even when taxying, was about as popular in the area as a brass band in a Trappist monastery. Protests, both public and personal, filled the Press, the post and the telephone exchange. I fully sympathized with them, but I had a job to do, as I tried to explain. I remained subject to complaints, appeals, abuse and threats. Some of the latter really went too far and one from a neighbouring farmer, whom we will call Kane, finally tipped the balance of my tolerance. I invited my old friend the Malling police sergeant to see what he could do, short of formal legal action; and he bicycled off to call on Mr Kane.

' Afternoon, Mr Kane, Sir. Afraid I've come to see you on rather an awkward matter. It's this letter here, Sir, addressed to the Group Captain at the airfield which purports to come from you. May I ask if in fact you wrote it? '

' Let's have a look. Yes of course I did—meant everything I said in it too.'

' But, Sir, what about this last paragraph of yours? Constitutes a direct threat of lethal violence to the person, doesn't it? You surely can't pretend you don't know that's illegal?'

Mr Kane was genuinely surprised. 'Of course I know it's illegal as far as ordinary people are concerned—but does it really apply to the RAF too?'

He apparently thought there was some sort of open season, as for vermin. There was little to be done about it; but at least I cancelled his honorary membership of our Officers' Mess. I felt he couldn't have it both ways—and after all he probably wouldn't want to associate with our sort of people anyway.

The general outcry about the local noise situation became so serious, however, that the RAF Director General of Public Relations, the well known and well loved Gus Walker, made the unusual decision that a Press Open Day should be held at West Malling, to try to clarify the situation and improve relationships. The national and local papers were invited to attend and their representatives turned up in large numbers. We spent the morning showing them around the Station and the aircraft, explaining operational requirements and procedures, and demonstrating that every precaution possible was taken to reduce noise level and nuisance, eg no flying after midnight, no practice airfield circuits but direct approaches from a very high altitude radar collecting-point down to the runway, large and expensive bafflers to deaden the sound of engine tests and so on. After a good lunch, we had an hour and more's discussion at which everyone could and did air their views. I summed up much as follows: 'Well, gentlemen, I hope we've given you what you came for and that we've been able to convince you that we make no unnecessary noise, indeed only the inevitable minimum; that we really are leaning over backwards to minimize the noise we do have to make. Perhaps you can persuade your readers of this—and that it honestly is no good ringing me up at all hours asking us to make less noise. We just can't'.

Next day I made the headlines in the Daily Mirror—'Air Chief says Don't ring me up'. At least they made me an 'Air chief' some 11 years prematurely. I learnt a salutary lesson for the future: when speaking to the Press, don't.

The next year, however, all these problems were resolved by the decision once again to close West Malling; or in fact, rather surprisingly, to transfer it progressively to the United States Navy for transport operations. The US Navy proved an admirable bunch of people, the only drawback being that it took the RAF a little time to realize that American spirituous liquor is very much stronger by proof than our own. While I was still occupying the CO's quarter our new Navy friends were honoured by a visit of inspection from Commander Douglas Fairbanks Jr, USNR. He was not of course concerned with the RAF side of things, and it was only by coincidence that I met him being seen off at Malling railway station that evening. I was going to London on a private visit and we agreed to share a compartment.

The only slight awkwardness was that I had purchased myself a second-class ticket. However, I naturally joined him in a first-class compartment, and, when the ticket inspector appeared, with some embarrassment duly paid over the difference in fare. A moment later it was with perhaps a little more embarrassment that Commander Fairbanks had to do the same.

With some apprehension, I now found myself once again at the feet of the Air Secretary. Once again he passed me deftly to the Jolly Jokers department of his organization. In July 1960 I was told at short notice that, together with my friends Colonel Phillip Tower and Captain Ian McGeogh RN, I had been selected for the American National War College. This was a real honour because foreign students had been excluded for many years after the Fuchs and Pontecorvo security scandals, and presumably the British authorities would be keen to re-establish their good name by sending of their best. However, in short order the story of our selection was prematurely leaked to the American Press; all the other NATO countries clamoured for vacancies also; and Secretary for Defence Gates took fright and cancelled the whole deal.

This news reached us at the last possible moment when we were literally packed for the boat, had made all personal arrangements for a tour overseas and disposed of goods and chattels, including for one of us his home. I only had the slightly awkward experience of having to go down and dicker with a highly suspicious car dealer in Maidstone to buy back the car I had sold him the previous week (at least I knew its history). Quite justifiably he charged me the full commission. This gave rise to an interesting example of inter-Service non-standardization. We three hapless victims made financial claims to the three separate Service Ministries that then still existed. The Captain, after much official tooth-sucking, was finally awarded £250; I received £28; and the gallant Colonel got nothing (' exigencies of the Service, my dear fellow '). At least I was placed second.

Some official conscience must have been stirred by our misfortunes because a genuinely special effort was now made on our behalf. The normal intake of students at the British Imperial Defence College was raised by three and we were granted vacancies to take effect the following January, about five months hence. In the interval to keep me out of mischief I was sent to the Senior Officers War Course (SOWC) at Greenwich, where I learned a great deal; made some lifelong friends; enjoyed the splendidly traditional atmosphere; and drank a lot of gin, thus earning the official title of graduates from the establishment ' Old Soak '.

One of the notable advantages of such courses lies in the opportunities provided to learn and understand more about one's sister Services; some of the experiences are distinctly unexpected. The SOWC was by no means the only inter-Service course current at Greenwich; there were several others, at various rank levels and in many fields of training.

Two RAF flight lieutenants on a joint tactical course decided to relax on the town one evening; booked themselves a couple of theatre tickets; and proceeded to the College Main Gate. There their exit was barred by a Chief Petty Officer of commanding and majestic mien.

' Sorry, gentlemen. Can't leave now. Liberty boat's just gone.'

' What d'you mean "liberty boat", Chief? We're not going to sea, we're just catching a bus to the West End.'

' Ah, yes, Sir, but not just now, I'm afraid. You see we've got a traditional custom here; based on the old liberty boat runs from a ship lying off, it is. Boats run at quarter to and quarter past the hour, and them's the only times you can leave, see? Afraid you'll have to wait twenty-five minutes for the next boat.'

' But we shall miss our theatre.'

' Sorry, Sir, can't help that—regulations is regulations.'

The RAF officers retired muttering in the direction of the ward-room; but a few minutes later reappeared at the gate. This time they were barefoot, carrying their shoes and socks.

' Still twenty minutes to the next boat, gentlemen ', pronounced its guardian.

' That's all right, Chief. We've decided not to bother with the boat this time—we're going to paddle ashore '.

And they suited the action to the word.

The Imperial Defence College also proved interesting and valuable, fulfilling its designed purpose of giving one time to think, to read and to debate; and thus acquire a broader and deeper outlook on and knowledge of world affairs. In mid-course I was promoted Air Commodore and really had little cause for complaint when some bitters were added to my cup by receiving the appointment, after three earlier abortive essays by the Jolly Jokers Department, of Director of Organization and Administrative Plans in the Air Ministry, Whitehall. This was about as onerous and laborious a job as it sounds but was all part of a sensible policy to try out aspirant officers in such a field to see if they continue to pull their weight.

In a book which aims to keep the reader entertained, perhaps only two incidents are worth recording from the somewhat routine period that followed.

One day I was operating studiously but perhaps rather discontentedly at my Ministry desk when a Loose Minute found its way to the top of my In Tray. It referred to the RAF's participation in the annual Festival of Remembrance at the Albert Hall. The Hall's structural format, with its lofty domed roof and small access doors, more or less confined such participation to the human element of the Services. We had in succession displayed the Colour Squadron, the precision drill squad, the WRAF band, the gymnastic apprentices and the RAF Police with their dogs. Had any addressees of the Loose Minute any other bright ideas?

Now at this time there was considerable dissatisfaction in the RAF arising from the fact that many officers had reached Very High Rank at an unusually early age; and consequently were now processing in a stately pavane round the available senior appointments. Retirements were few and general promotion prospects consequently not bright. In the mood of the moment, I scrawled rather rudely across the paper ' Why don't the Air Council put on their well-known display of musical chairs? ' and tossed it without further thought into the Out Tray.

I had not taken due account of the conscientiousness of the Civil Servant, in this case my admirable lady Personal Assistant. A week or so later I was

114

electrified to read another widely circularized Minute. It read: 'Festival of Remembrance. The following suggestions from the sources listed have been received in reply to our loose minute reference . . . Final selection from them will shortly be made by the Participation Committee'. Suggestion (iv) read: 'Musical Chairs by the Air Council—Director of Organization and Administrative Plans'.

I spent a frenzied but eventually successful morning tearing round the Ministry and recovering the incriminating copies; but a few more grey hairs duly developed.

By this time I had, over the years, been doing quite a lot of writing. A few short stories and BBC scripts; but the great majority for Service and professional publications. I had some successes in prize essay competitions, and wrote regularly for Brassey's Annual, the Royal United Services Journal and the RAF Quarterly. My contributions to the latter were generally lighthearted. In 1962 I invented a fictional Civil Servant, one Horace Slapcabbage, whose doings were regularly described in that journal. The humour was unmalicious, indeed somewhat juvenile. Perhaps I may be allowed to quote an example. Lord Slapcabbage, by now ennobled as so many of his fellows in an attempt to reduce his damage-potential, has been chairing a Royal Commission on the Rationalization of the Armed Forces; he is being interviewed on his report by a journalist:

J: I understand, my lord, that your report includes some proposals on the integration of the Chaplaincy Services?

LS: It does indeed. We considered that the present system is cumbrous, complicated and wasteful of men and money—to say nothing of cloth, eh?

J: But, my lord, have not previous attempts been made in this direction and proved unworkable?

LS: True enough. But this time I have proposed a novel and more radical approach. We recommend that all Church of England servicemen and women should be in the Army; all Roman Catholics in the Navy; and all Other Denominations, as they are called—Methodists and so on—in the Royal Air Force. Thus at a stroke, we attain the desired objective —one branch of Chaplain for each branch of the Service. Simple but effective, I flatter myself.

J: But, Lord Slapcabbage, haven't you forgotten the non-Christians; Jews, Muslims, atheists, agnostics and so on? Will they not be able to join under your plan?

LS: What d'you think the Marines are for, my boy?

As I say, lighthearted stuff; and, as I imagined, inoffensive. I was wrong. Some time after the emergence of Clapcabbage, I was sent for by my master, Air Vice Marshal Kiwi Broughton. After discussing certain routine professional matters I rose to leave his office.

'There's one other thing, Christopher. Slapcabbage. I've been requested to ask you to stop writing about him.'

I was flabbergasted. 'What? Requested? By whom?'

' By certain of our civil service colleagues.'

I exploded in predictable fury, mouthing of freedom of speech, Fascist censorship, pompous self-importance and so on. Kiwi patiently heard me out.

' Yes, yes, of course I knew you'd react like that; and of course you're quite right. But look at it this way. How much d'you get for these literary efforts? Three guineas a time? Just think—is it really worth for that amount alienating all these people who, like it or not, you're going to have to work with and keep on good terms with for a dozen years? '

He was, as usual, right. I conceded the point; and Slapcabbage duly died. But not without some memorial. I inserted an obituary notice for him in The Times: ' Slapcabbage, Horace—suddenly in Whitehall on 2 January. No flowers or letters please '.

It cost me, by coincidence, three guineas; but the story may someday have a happy ending. Years later when the sanction of Civil Service disapproval perhaps weighed less heavily on me, I came across some letters from Lord Slapcabbage to his son, à la mode de Lord Chesterfield. They are as yet unpublished—but who knows?

With such a troubled passage through the swamps of Whitehall, it was not entirely without apprehension that in the early spring of 1963 I received summons to the office of the Chief of Air Staff, my old mentor Sir Thomas Pike. Which of my sins had found me out?

None, it transpired. This was 1943 in reverse. Now it was ' For "court martial" read "promotion" throughout '. I was to become, with immediate effect, Air Vice Marshal, Assistant Chief of Defence Staff.

16 'There is a tide in the affairs of men'

It could not have been a more fascinating time to join the Central Defence Staff, whose hierarchy consisted of the Chief of Defence Staff, the Vice Chief and the Assistant Chief, one from each of the three Services. Until recently the authority and responsibilities of the Central Staff had been restricted and somewhat nebulous. Its location in Storey's Gate, musty and murky, smacked of Victorian bureaucracy rather than the corridors of contemporary power. Now the CDS, in the person of Lord Mountbatten, and the Secretary of State, Peter Thorneycroft, were pressing ahead with a programme which its proponents described as rationalization, functionalization or integration, to taste; its opponents referred to it as ' all power to the Centre ', ' the take-over bid ', or more bluntly ' The Power Grab '. The lines of battle were drawn and the warriors of Whitehall sniffed at its scent and pawed their pending trays in keen anticipation.

My own arrival on this scene was attributable to the fact that my old friend Air Vice Marshal Donald Evans was to be moved sideways into a newly created appointment, designed to be the spearhead of the new arrangements, Chief Staff Officer for Defence Re-Organisation. I took his place as Assistant Chief, so in effect the CDS had created two Air Vice Marshals where God had only created one. This caused considerable initial confusion, especially since, presumably in view of the amount of hostility generated against the new organization, much of the activity in the Central Staffs appeared to proceed within an impenetrable and somewhat ridiculous cloak of secrecy. This was well illustrated when, after a couple of weeks of inextricable disorder and misunderstanding between Donald Evans' department and my own, I approached the Chief Information Officer of the Ministry to ask if a Press release could not be made to clarify the situation. This office was at the time held by a splendid retired brigadier of the classic mould, one Godfrey Hobbs.

' Yes, yes ', he said, ' I see the difficulty over your new appointment. Tell you what—I'll leak it to *The Times* '.

Perhaps naively, I replied, ' But Godfrey, why "leak" it? Can't we just straightforwardly tell them—after all, there's nothing undercover about it '.

It was clearly a novel idea to him. The corridors of MOD power were at the time about as straightforward as a left-handed corkscrew, and every ball bowled down them came out of the back of the hand (' Right you are, Freddie, we'll fix it that way. Tip the wink to Henry and Charlie but better leave Eric out of this one. His turn next time, maybe '). Hence the suggestion of a direct transmission of information to the Press, without circumvention or camouflage, came as a nasty shock to the CIO. However, to do him credit, he accepted the point, bit the bullet and issued a public explanatory statement of the new set-up.

Unhappily immediately thereafter everything went back into the melting pot when Donald Evans was stricken with a serious internal illness and had to retire from active duty for some considerable time. This left me responsible for both jobs, and I acquired the simple and easily intelligible title of ' Assistant Chief of Defence Staff (General) and Chief Staff Officer for Defence Re-Organisation '.

The Central Staffs and indeed the whole defence scene were at this time dominated by Lord Mountbatten of whose record, talents and personality enough has been said and written without my presuming to add anything here. With the support of Sir Solly (now Lord) Zuckerman and the Permanent Under Secretary of State, Sir Henry Hardman, and with of course his own royal and international connections, he bestrode the narrow world of defence like a Colossus; and of course was a powerful and influential figure in the nation's affairs, perhaps the last such military man who will emerge in our history.

A senior appointment in the Central Defence Staff in those days was not wholly enviable. Lord Mountbatten made it quite clear to me in our initial interview that he did not expect me to loosen my connections with my own Service, rather that he wished me to act as his go-between with it and general fount of information about its activities and aspirations. In view of the suspicion in which Central Staff officers were sometimes held, this was easier said than done. My own experience was rather unusual. In my early days in office I was brash enough to become involved in some differences of opinion with his lordship and Sir Solly. The fact that initially I was thus clearly persona not particularly grata with the Central hierarchy made me gratissima with the RAF authorities, who seemed to regard me in the guise of a dedicated champion prepared to defend their special interests to the last gasp. In due course however my Central superiors and I contrived to understand each other better and good relations blossomed. Promptly in consequence I became gravely suspect in RAF circles, as a sort of turncoat; doors were closed to me and it became more difficult to do an effective job.

There were nevertheless many and interesting duties to be done. Apart from the functional re-organisation programme, ACDS was something of a general Defence dogsbody, factotum or perhaps waste-paper basket. Whenever anything unusual or off-beat cropped up it seemed to arrive on my plate, whether it was the task of deflating a ridiculous concept of basing NATO's deterrent on internationally-manned missile-launching merchant ships; proprietorial and self-interested squabbles in NATO; or defence arrangements with newly independent ex-colonial territories.

In the latter field I was privileged to make several trips abroad with Mr Duncan Sandys, by then the Secretary of State for Commonwealth Relations and Colonial Affairs. Not renowned for his tolerance or sweetness of temper, he nevertheless proved a most interesting and entertaining travelling companion, any critical onslaughts he launched being directed at the representatives of his own Ministry. We did have one notable contre-

118

temps. We had taken off from London Airport in a VIP Comet of the Royal Air Force. Our destination was Aden where the usual troubles were brewing with both locals and neighbours, including some unusual ones such as the decapitation of unfortunate captured British soldiers. We were to refuel at El Adem in Libya, involving an initial flight of four hours.

After an early supper on board, we were sitting in the lounge of the aircraft playing Canasta, a game to which the Secretary of State was addicted. He did not like being interrupted during its progress, so, when the captain of the aircraft appeared in our midst, he dismissed him somewhat abruptly. The captain, however, an officer of Polish extraction, declined to be so dismissed and insisted on having his say.

' Well, if you must—but out with it, man. Can't you see we're busy? '

' Sir, it is a bomb. We have report from London Airport. They received a telephone message a bomb has been placed in our aircraft.'

' Well, don't bother me. Get your people to have a look for it.'

' Sir, if the bomb is as stated in luggage hold, we cannot search in flight. Sir, do you wish me to return to London Airport? '

The Secretary of State turned to me. ' That's not for me to say, surely. You're the senior officer on board. Tell him what to do.'

Strictly speaking it was not up to me either. The captain's authority in flight is paramount and the decision should be his, although he had been quite right to consult his VIP passengers. However, I felt he needed some help so we put our heads together. Our flight time was an estimated four hours and we were already one and a half hours en route. So, if we turned back, we would be at risk for a further one and a half hours; if we went on, two and a half. I thought the extra hour was a reasonable bet and told the captain so. We pressed on; but somehow the standard of Canasta seemed to drop off a bit thereafter.

The bomb threat turned out to be a hoax. Search at El Adem revealed no bomb. It was unfortunate however that on the nine o'clock news the BBC told its listeners about the telephone call, since my wife was one of them. Service wives have to learn to take the rough with the smooth, but this was a little rougher than usual.

Another trip in company with Mr Sandys took us to Uganda (the pre-Amin version, of course), Kenya and Tanzania. All were newly emergent states, and had many arrangements including defence to make in consultation with the late colonial power. Spice was added to this particular trip by the mutinies that had broken out in the local armies. Our assistance over these was needed and requested, but of course had to be discreet in view of national sensitivities. It was a successful tour, and it was fascinating meeting the leading political personalities, who to me at least had till then been names in the news or pictures in the Press.

The defence talks with the Kenyan authorities were conducted in a generally friendly and relaxed atmosphere. The Kenyan negotiating team was personally led by Jomo Kenyatta, the Prime Minister, and included other familiar names such as Mboya, Odinga and Nguru. Our side was of course led by Mr Sandys, with myself in uniform as the senior British military representative. One of the requirements stated by the Kenyans was for an effective and comprehensive air defence system, justified they claimed by Russian aircraft having been supplied to their unfriendly neighbour Somalia. Mr Sandys was concerned that the full financial implications of such a proposal might not be appreciated.

' Mr Prime Minister, I naturally sympathize with your wish to defend your country and your airspace; but I am worried about the great expense you will inevitably incur if you embark on the sort of programme you have in mind. As you are aware, I was myself until quite recently Secretary of State for Defence in my own country. Of all the vast costs involved in modern sophisticated armed forces, no element is more forbiddingly expensive than air defence. Everything about it is expensive. Not just the fighter aircraft themselves, but the necessary radar and ground control systems, the servicing and repair facilities, the fuel and the special runways, the armaments and electronic equipments. Even a fighter pilot himself is a very costly commodity.'

He turned to me.

' Tell us, Air Marshal, how much does it cost to train a jet fighter pilot?'

' Secretary of State, it's not easy to give you a precise figure. It all depends on what you include in the bill for the individual pilot, for example a proportion of the cost of the initial training aircraft purchase, its amortization and so on. But at the lowest a trained Service pilot will cost the wrong side of £100,000.' (This was in 1964—it would be treble that now.)

This statement produced a considerable hush. During it, Tom Mboya who was sitting opposite me eyed me carefully up and down. He then turned to his neighbour and commented sotto voce (only not too sotto): ' I wouldn't give a hundred thousand for him, would you?'

I had to admit he had a point.

Such overseas expeditions made a welcome break in what was otherwise not a wholly enjoyable appointment. The Champs de Whitehall have never been my favourite pastures, especially now that I was more or less their head groundsman. It was therefore with some relief that I learned that I was once again to be short-toured. What happened was that my immediate superior, and wise counsellor and friend, the Vice Chief, General Rory O'Connor, was on tour expiry replaced by an Air Marshal. This disturbed the inter-Service symmetry of the Central Staff; and I, after only 15 months as Assistant Chief, was to be replaced by a Major-General. Yet another interview with the Air Secretary awaited me. This time I was to be a highly satisfied customer.

The centre of activity for our armed forces had once again reverted to the Far East, where renewed troubles had broken out. Casting a casual glance at their wall atlases, the wizards of Whitehall had proposed a new state of Malaysia, comprising what had been the colonial territories of Malaya, Singapore and North Borneo. The very considerable ethnological, cultural and economic differences between these countries did not disturb them unduly; after all the countries were geographically reasonably adjacent. The new arrangement did however considerably antagonize the Indonesians,

120

who did not relish the establishment to their immediate north of a major power which they suspected would eventually be dominated by its non-Muslim Chinese element of population; furthermore it pre-empted their own territorial ambitions in Borneo. They decided to oppose it, to use their own curious phrase, to confront it.

Confrontation ('confrontazi') was the order of the day, and it was preceded by an internal revolt in the North Borneo state of Brunei, which had in fact declined to join Malaysia. The Sultan appealed for British help, due to him under treaty obligations; and, in view of growing 'confrontazi', so shortly afterwards did the Malaysian authorities. We had firm commitments and decided to honour them. This of course would mean major activity for all three Services and considerable reinforcements for the area.

The RAF's organization in the Far East consisted of the Far East Air Force itself, with an Air Marshal Air Commander under an overall joint C-in-C. The Air Commander conducted local operations through his Tactical Force, No 224 Group, commanded by an Air Vice Marshal. This latter job rotated between the Royal Australian Air Force, who made a sizeable contribution to its strength, and the RAF; the Royal New Zealand Air Force provided the Senior Air Staff Officer for the Group, again commensurate with its own force contribution. At this critical time a new Air Commander was appointed in the person of Air Marshal Peter Wykeham (né Wykeham-Barnes, he had recently reverted to the single name). He was in my opinion, and that of many others, the outstanding RAF officer of my generation; he was a man of great operational skill, courage and experience as demonstrated in both World War II and Korea; of deep intelligence and broad culture; and of considerable personal charm. Consequently he was the ideal choice for his appointment and I noted with anxious interest, shared by my contemporaries, that the job of AOC 224 Group would shortly fall to the RAF's turn again. I mentioned this in my interview with the Air Secretary.

'Of course, I do realize that one can't always be given exactly what one wants but perhaps it might help you in your deliberations on my future to know what I *do* want. What I would like most of all is to be AOC 224 Group under Pete Wykeham. I . . .'

He cut me short. 'That's all right. He's already asked for you. When can you be ready to go?'

I left his office on a small rosy cloud and, pausing only to pick up my equally delighted wife, caught the first P&O steamship to our beloved Singapore.

Much proved to have changed there since we had left eight years before, but much was unchanged and unchanging. There had been considerable political developments. Singapore had attained its independence, for the time being as a partner state of Malaysia. The practical effect on the British forces stationed there by agreement was that we were no longer our own masters, operating only under the direct orders of our own government. We were now guests, invited and made welcome but nevertheless guests in a foreign country. We acted in co-operation with the governments of the various components of Malaysia and co-ordinated our operations with those of their armed forces; but we were no longer the military monarchs of all we surveyed, and initially often had to remind ourselves of this.

My wife and I were now naturally officially and handsomely housed, in the AOC's official residence in the northern sector of Singapore City. The house was in the old colonial style, high and airy, and with quarters for a large staff. By accepted convention the drivers were Muslim Malays, the household staff Chinese and the gardeners Indian or Tamil. It is fashionable now to decry such staffs and their service; but I can only say that they were loyal, efficient, industrious and happy—and especially that they apparently found no difficulty in their microcosm of a multi-racial and multi-religious state, an example from which other and more important people might well benefit. The Number One Boy ('Sir, you are my seventh AOC') was a man of great character, dignity and of much valuable common sense. On one occasion, on my return from leave in Hong Kong he reported all in order but commented on the unusual phenomenon of a Canberra aircraft making some low passes over the house. I explained matters.

'Oh, yes, Ah Chow—I should have told you. I asked the photographic squadron to take the opportunity of any flying they were doing around here to take a picture of the house for the official Christmas card. That would account for it.'

'No, Sir, do not think that. No take photograph—no stop.'

My operational Headquarters was at Seletar on the Johore Straight and my two main Singapore bases were there and at Tengah; there were others in Malaya, the largest being the mainly Australian base at Butterworth opposite Penang Island. But with the intensification of Confrontation the weight of operations and consequently of our deployment shifted more and more to Borneo and our smaller bases there at Kuching, Sibu, Labuan, Tawan and so on. As the tempo of operations increased more and more reinforcements poured into 224 Group, which reached a strength of over 300 aircraft. It became a comprehensive airforce in miniature comprising almost every type of operational aircraft. As before in the Malayan Emergency it was the mobility and logistic flexibility provided by the air transport component that gave us the winning card in the game. Our troops in Borneo depended on the Hastings, the Beverley and the NZ Freighters for air dropped supply to enable them to reach and hold otherwise impossible positions in the jungle-covered mountains of Borneo. The helicopters, Belvedere and Whirlwind, together with a naval contribution of Wessex particularly valuable for their greater load lift, supplemented the supply and provided the mobility to overcome the impenetrability of the jungle—although I should stress that by now many of our seasoned troops were just as skilful there as their indigenous opponents, often even more so since the latter were often themselves of indifferent quality.

During this period I was shot at by an enemy for the first time in 20 years. This was quite a regular experience for the crews supply dropping to our forward troops, whose positions were often so close to the frontier that the aircraft involved were within small arms range from Indonesian territory, to say nothing of bands of enemy infiltrators. I found my reaction rather unexpected. As usual, 1 was frightened but I was also indignant in a ludicrously self-important way. I felt an overwhelming urge to lean out of the cock-pit and shout: ' Watch it there, you ignorant clods. D'you realize there's a respectable middle-aged Air Vice Marshal you're shooting at. Now behave yourselves and mind your manners '.

It may indeed surprise some readers that a middle-aged Air Vice Marshal should be engaged in such activity, but it should not surprise anyone who has served in the RAF. I have always tried to make it a principle to have no aircraft under my command which I have not flown, or, perhaps more importantly, been seen to fly. This is not to suggest that one can fly everything under command—I had more than 20 aircraft types in 224 Group—competently and operationally. Apart from any natural defects one may have developed over the years, there just isn't time do to so. But I believe most strongly that the young men flying aircraft under a commander must observe that he has at least tried it out. Not that there is anything inspirational about this—quite the reverse. The young men concerned fly their aircraft with great skill and confidence and see no reason why others should not do the same. It has been well said that a junior officer watching his commander take-off has only one or two thoughts on the matter, ' I hope the old bastard doesn't break his neck ' (if he likes him); or ' I hope he *does* break his neck ' (if the reverse applies).

No; the thinking behind my policy and practice was simply that I considered that no senior officer should ever be in a position of administering a rebuke, verbal or written, to one of his pilots for flying error, if the young man concerned can say to himself ' How does he know, the silly old fossil? He's never even flown one of the damn things '.

So—one flies the damn things; and for the most part it is all very enjoyable.

The development of this war was somewhat unexpected, as were some of its secondary effects. Those who were sent out to reinforce knew what they were in for; those who had come out before 1964 found a comfortably routine tour of peacetime duty suddenly and unexpectedly converted into a demanding, often hazardous and nearly always uncomfortable period of active service. Almost without exception the men of all three Services reacted splendidly; and after some initial errors and hesitations due to inexperience proved as good or better men as their fathers and grandfathers (I did however have one odd case of two young airmen called on to serve in the dense jungle who, city born and bred, proved to have a quite genuine terror of the darkness). The men's wives, often no more than teenagers, sometimes did less well. Reared in the bosom of the Welfare State, with Mum or Gran always on call when needed, they did not manage their unexpected grass-widowhood very well, often proving vague, helpless and plaintive and demanding a great deal of care and attention from people who could ill spare the time.

There were of course plenty of exceptions to this generalization. We had to maintain all-weather fighters in Borneo to patrol the airspace and deter or intercept the occasional enemy intrusion. Apart from some major paradrops in Malaya, there was little of this but the job had to be done. A rota system was introduced by which each such aircrew did one month unaccompanied in Borneo, two months back at his home base in Singapore or Malaya, and then off again to Borneo. Many of these people were old hands who had served with me at West Malling and Stradishall, sometimes not much younger than myself. I was dancing one evening with the sonsy Scots wife of one of these, a woman in her forties whom I had known well for some years.

' I'm a bit worried about folk like you and Bob, Jeannie ', I observed. ' It's all very well for the dashing youngsters but I reckon it's a bit rough for people like yourselves to have to face these repeated and unexpected separations.'

' Rough? ' she replied. ' Nonsense, quite the reverse. I tell you, I'm getting four honeymoons a year at my time of life—marvellous! '

The good ones will always turn up trumps.

Of course, our relationships with the Army were close and good. They had to be because we were so interdependent that we could not afford to let each other down. The soldier (or airman or even sailor) had a pretty unpleasant time in the jungle even when there were no human enemies about. He reacted traditionally. He swore; and he coped. But he was not always quite sure of his position.

The trouble was that we had to convince so-called world opinion that right was on our side (which it was) and that it was a matter of the Malaysians defending their home land against the aggression of Indonesia (which they were). If it were known that the majority of the soldiers and sailors and nearly all the airmen conducting the defence were in fact British, Australian or New Zealanders, the anti-colonialist clique which has always constituted one of the less appealing aspects of the United Nations would have started up their usual ill-informed and unattractive clamour, and might even have damaged our chances of finishing things off quickly and cleanly. Thus when a successful encounter with the enemy was announced, the success was attributed to Malaysian Security Forces; and many a Cockney or Welshman enquired of his officer, ' Can you tell me, Sir—am I a member of the Malaysian Security Forces? '

Nevertheless on the whole the men had no doubt that they were doing a good professional job; a necessary job; and a morally justified job. Their faith was sometimes assailed by ignorant but earnest pacifists; and also on occasion by malevolent and near-subversive politicians from our own Parliament who sought to find some improvement of their own public image by demanding that of our troops. One such, himself a Scot, was overheard interrogating a sergeant of the Argylls in a forward jungle position: ' Now, Sergeant, do you really understand what this war's all about? Do you think it right for us to be out here getting mixed up in other people's local quarrels? Can you tell me just what you and your men are here for—what's the object of it all? '

' Sorr! ' came the crisp and sonorous reply. ' We are here to keep out the Communists—and all other left-wing bastards.'

124

And keep them out they did, most handsomely and impressively. Their Commander, the Director of Borneo Operations, George Lea and his charming wife became our close friends and whenever possible I included their lovely house in Brunei in my journeyings. Apart from the pleasure of their own company, they were great animal lovers, and there was always some fascinating new creature with whom to make friends. Best of all perhaps was Wilbur, a hornbill of great character and charm, among whose party pieces was the practice of flying onto the guardroom roof and turning out the guard with a wonderfully realistic imitation of the NCO's customary screech of command.

My wife took to the jungle like a duck to water. Apart from such comparatively routine activities as a safari in the Malayan National Park, she became a great afficionado of the long houses of Borneo, their inhabitants and indeed their rice wine; of which she is now an accepted connoisseur, although it unfortunately left her with an amoebic infection to which she is still recurrently subject. There can be few more fascinating areas of the world open to the enquiring mind to this day. One of our happiest memories is of the grand up-river regatta at Murubi where the average tribal crew would have baffled even my good friend John Snagge, since they rowed facing the wrong (or natural) way; numbered anything between thirty and sixty per boat to taste, with the ladies' crews presenting a most fearsome spectacle of topless liberated endeavour; long cigars were de rigueur for either sex when competing in the top class; and I once timed an enthusiastic crew at 114 strokes to the minute.

Since this does not essay to be an accurate military history, I will not go into a full chronological account of the war. We won; and we won effectively and finally in about two years. The contrast to the unhappy, unending story of Vietnam is of course striking. If I were asked to explain it, I would say that a fundamental cause lay in the fact that nearly all the inhabitants of Malaysia and especially those of Borneo wanted us to win; they hated the idea of occupation or even overlording by the Indonesians, with whom their enmity was deep-seated and traditional. Whereas in Vietnam, as I and many others saw it, the root cause for the French and American débacles was the average Vietnamese simply did not give a damn which side won, if only he personally could be left alone. If he had to join in on one side or the other, all he was interested in was being on the winning side; some turned their coats at least six times in futile attempts to accomplish this. I do not suggest for a moment that the average Dayak tribesman was really pro-British or even pro-Malaysian; but he realized where his best interests lay and in so doing made a major contribution to their attainment.

So what proved impossible for the French and the Americans in Vietnam and very arduous for ourselves in the earlier Malayan Emergency, was on this occasion accomplished in a comparatively brief campaign. Above all it was classically cost effective. The object of the exercise, as they teach at staff colleges, was attained and attained with a laudable economy of effort, and in particular casualties. Over a period of two years the total casualties sustained by the eventually large 'Malaysian Security Forces', in both

125

killed and wounded, did not reach one thousand combatants; and there were no massacres, no misdirected bombings, no doctrinaire butcheries of the non-combatant. At the end of it all, we felt we had done rather well and had some cause for self-satisfaction. When the time came for the Secretary of State for Defence, Mr Denis Healey, to make his statement on the campaign and its successful conclusion to the House of Commons, we sat back perhaps rather smugly awaiting the thanks and plaudits of our masters.

' Tsk, tsk! ' in effect said the ineffable Mr Healey, ' we must never get involved in that sort of lark again. Much too expensive for our station in life '.

As a comment, it certainly qualified for the Non-inspirational Oscar of the year. Perhaps we had been naive to expect anything else.

I stayed on in Singapore for about six months after the campaign was over, supervising the rather sad process of the deflation of my command. Apart from the perfectly justifiable removal of our ad hoc reinforcements, inter-governmental negotiations got under way for our eventual total military withdrawal at an originally remote date but one which seemed to be advanced every time the Chancellor of the Exchequer rattled his piggy-bank. There were political crises also as Singapore broke from Malaysia and Mr Lee Kwan Yew set about the challenging task of establishing it as a wholly independent island state. Thus when the time came to leave again in March 1967, it was in an atmosphere of general as well as personal sadness. The pipe and drum band of 224 Group played our ship off in the dusk, and as she slid past the end of the quay, a lone piper played ' Will ye no come back again? ' It did not seem likely; we both wept unashamedly.

My professional future had been explained to me by the Chief of Air Staff, Sir Charles Elworthy, during a visit the previous year. His plan was that I should return to the dreaded Ministry of Defence to serve for about a year as Director General of Organization (RAF), under Kiwi Broughton once again; and then take the latter's place on the Air Council as Air Member for Supply and Organization. It was not an altogether attractive programme, but as AMSO I would be promoted Air Marshal, so at least there was some bright-ness on the horizon as we left our island home.

But before I take up the story again in London, perhaps I may be allowed to make a detour to another island which has played almost as large and happy a part in our lives as Singapore.

17 Grecian Idyll

I suppose subconsciously I was always oriented towards Greece. A prolonged classical education from the age of eight to twenty-one had given me a deep and lasting interest in its thought and history; while serving in the Middle East Squadrons I had seen many Aegean dawns and days, each more beautiful than the last; and my brief impression of Athens during its liberation further whetted my appetite and interest. On a certain morning in May 1963 I was travelling on the Underground to my duties in Whitehall and met an old friend, an Army Colonel. I commented on his striking suntan.

'Where have you been, Mike, to get so splendidly brown? Ski-ing in Austria?'

'No, no—we've just come back from our Greek island, Skiathos.'

By the time we got off at Westminster, I was more or less hooked. By the time I looked into the prospect a little further, I was lost. I purchased an acre or more of land at very low cost and opened negotiations with a British architect living in happy exile on the island.

I had never been that far north in the Aegean and consequently had never even seen Skiathos, which lies just off the eastern coast of Greece, opposite Volos and above the big island of Euboea. Skiathos is almost unique among Aegean islands in being well watered and therefore gloriously and luxuriantly green, mountainous but not barren or rocky since the hills are covered in all manner of trees, wild and cultivated, heather, broom and flowers. There are 71 sandy beaches on the island; in 1963 there were 36 outsiders there, so that worked out at about two beaches each; and even now almost empty beaches can quite easily be found, particularly by boat. Although by now unhappily better known to the tourist trade, at that time it was scarcely heard of and the only information available about it other than by word of mouth was included in an irresistible locally produced pamphlet entitled 'Touristic Informations'. I quote some extracts:

On arrival, an amusing ready-to-serve GANG of young and old will arrange everyone in a short time.

Meals are obtainable at accessible prices, and there are many neat Tavernes with local colours which have inspired very much the great Papadiamantis and two pastry shops at the Quay, where you will find several kinds of pastries and sweets, the renowned BAKLAVA, Almond candies and during the first fortnight of August their famous Doughnuts.

127

There are also many Coffee Houses where you can drink the Ouzo, which is served with piquant tit-bits and delicious Octopus cooked into embers.

At Koukounaries with the golden seashore there are handy barracks where you will find momentary meals.

Visitors will have the opportunity to visit the famous MANDRAKI, a seashore on the north backside.

The memorial day of Aglios FANOURIOS is celebrated pompously, to the vigil even participating not only the natives but also strangers. Shrines are everywhere dispersed and beautiful altar screens scattered over sheltered beaches.

After all this we clearly had no choice but to make this our second home. We looked forward eagerly to our initial visit of reconnaissance in the Spring of 1964. But here it will be remembered the authorities played a hand and pointed me toward the Far East. I was therefore faced with the awkward alternatives of going ahead with building more or less blind, depending only on maps and architect's drawings, or postponing the whole project until probably 1967. Expert opinion was that the current very reasonable building costs would have doubled by then (they did, and have since trebled again), so I took the plunge and gave a green light to the builder, The latter, now a close friend, Nicos Andritsopoulos, was a recently demobilized young Greek army engineer and one became the victim of his apprentice hand at house building; but what emerged was enchantingly pretty, although bearing no apparent resemblance to either the architect's drawings or the builder's plans.

We managed to fit in a visit to our new home before leaving for the Far East. Our arrival unfortunately coincided not only with the downpours associated with the equinoctial change of season but also with some of the rare earthquakes to hit the island. As we should have expected, our house was not finished, having no driveway or access path inter alia, so we stayed the first few nights at Taki Dervenis' pub on the corner of the quay in the town. This also happened to be unfinished, lacking such refinements as the top storey. My wife's first night on an Aegean island was thus spent under a steady showerbath from the ceiling which ensured that she kept awake to watch the pictures stand out a foot or so from the wall as each tremor rocked us. She appeared unimpressed by the attractions of Greek life. The same hostelry was later the scene of our Builder's Party. On the completion (or near completion in our own case) of a house, there was a pleasant custom by which the new owner gave a party for those contributing to its construction, the architect, the electrician, the plumber, the carpenter and so on. I was of course happy to follow this custom and remained so even when I found that practically everyone on the island seemed to have been involved in the building, or at least was related to someone who had been, which was apparently good enough. There was no cause for concern, with prices as low as they were then; there was a considerable local shortage of bottles and my hazy memory tells me that the price of a bottle of retsina was four drachmas and one got five back on the empty—but I suppose I must be wrong. Anyway, it was a memorable party.

My wife continued to be somewhat baffled by the Greek way of social life, which of course to a large extent excludes the ladies. Dancing is a mainly male pursuit, but after she courteously accepted the sign-language invitation from an extremely intoxicated ancient at a neighbouring table to join him on the dance floor, it was too late to withdraw when, on lurching to the upright position, he proved to be one-legged. A one-legged drunken Greek pensioner can be a dangerous dancing partner, but everyone rallied cheerfully to her side (or his) and all went reasonably well. Later she was to be seen leading a sort of Hellenized conga line perilously close to the harbour's edge, arms locked with those of Nico and the chief of police. Her enthusiasm, and tomorrow's headache, were perhaps attributable to some confusion in her mind between *Ya Sou,* the normal toast, meaning merely ' Good Health ' and *Aspro Parto* which means ' Bottoms Up '.

We soon established some firm and lasting friendships. Names were a little difficult at first. The Greeks, like the Welsh, tend to identify by occupation, eg Paniotis the Water, and Manoli the Rubbish, to say nothing of another essential dometic expert known only as ' The Man for the Catastrophes ', I of course was Christo, but further identification proved difficult for the locals. Air Vice Marshals were naturally to them unknown phenomena but I did manage to get it across that I had some connection with the military.

This too led to misunderstanding. The people of Skiathos had happy memories of Her Majesty's forces. Before World War II the Mediterranean Fleet called there regularly on its annual cruise. Its archaic aircraft practiced a little genteel bombing and gunnery on allotted uninhabited islets. The Admiral led his officers and men ashore and took ceremonial refreshment with the Mayor. Ships were dressed overall, flags flew over the town and martial music was provided by the visitors on the quay. Thus, when I was drinking one evening with some of the senior members of Skiathos society at a waterfront café and attempting to establish communication, a happy smile of reminiscence illuminated the face of one sage. He pointed a gnarled finger at me.

' *Ah! esees* (you)! *Esees mereenban!* '

I was mystified.

' *Parakalo, then katalavaino* (I don't understand) '.

' *Esees* ' (much waving of arms and dramatic gesture), ' *esees mareenband* '.

I got it. He knew I had some military status and he had identified me; I was a retired conductor of the Marine Band. I was about to deny it regretfully when I thought to myself, ' Why not? Clearly retired conductors of the Marine Band are popular and welcome here. Why try to go into detailed explanation which no one will understand? Take a good offer when you get one '.

So I acknowledged his insight with a courteous lift of my glass; and for some years was known and well accepted in that role. Only later when my photograph began to appear in Greek newspapers as a NATO commander in chief was the deception detected; but nobody seemed to mind.

At that stage I spoke very little modern Greek. I had hoped that my ancient Greek would help, but it only did so in reading and writing, not in speaking or listening because the pronunciation is now so different. Even the words we have borrowed from the Greek which start with *auto* are not of much use because it has now become *afto*. *Basileus* (the King) has become *Vassilefs* and we have had to learn to call our neighbouring island Efvia instead of Euboea. My Greek has now improved a little but it is very much island Demotic; as was impressed on me later when as a NATO Commander I inspected the missile firing ranges established on the island of Crete. My Luftwaffe aircraft was met by the Greek admiral commanding the area, who unfortunately turned out not only to be important but also self-important. I greeted him in my best Skiathan, but he appeared somewhat taken aback. His aide drew mine aside.

' Please tell your master that, if that is all the Greek he knows, he had much better speak English.'

Rather pompous, really. After all, I had merely said ' Wotcher, me old mate—how's it going then? ', or words to that effect.

One bright morning on Skiathos I ran into my friend Nico Andritsopoulos, then I hasten to add a bachelor. He was not looking his handsome best and had clearly had a sleepless night. On enquiring I learned that he had been up all night playing poker. Poker is one of my own favourite pastimes so I asked if there was any chance of my sitting in on a game.

' No, I'm afraid not, Christo mou. You see your Greek isn't very fluent; we play special Greek rules; and in any case we play for very high stakes.'

I accepted the first two points but was not initially convinced by the third. These were not, after all, very rich men, fishermen, farmers, shop-keepers and so on. I suggested I should be able to match their comparatively modest wagers.

' Ah, no; you see, Christo, they don't just bet what cash they have—they will gamble with everything they possess. For example yesterday evening Costa owned most of the fishing fleet and Yanni Pandotis worked for him. Yanni had a lucky night and now it's the other way about—Costa's working for Yanni now.'

The Greeks are indeed great gamblers. When I had finished paying for my actual land and house I still owed a good deal of money locally for various services, painting, plumbing, electricity, decorating and of course all the furniture. I had brought out several hundreds of pounds worth of traveller's cheques intending to cash them to pay off the debts. At that time an added complication to such a process was that there were no actual bank branches in Skiathos. The various Greek banks sent representatives weekly to the island, who conducted business in any one of the larger local shops selected to taste.

As always I consulted the indispensable Taki. He located the man I wanted in the hardware store, and I gratefully accepted his offer to act as my interpreter over the deal. We were given the usual courteous welcome but it was soon quite clear that the travelling coffers did not contain the four or five hundred pounds worth of drachmas I required. A prolonged series of cups of metrio coffee followed while various emissaries popped in and out of the back door of the shop, gathering the necessary funds from here and there. At last the process was complete, the signed cheques were handed over and the money in return. As the last cup was emptied, the bank representative asked me a further question.

'What is he saying, Taki?' I asked.

'He wants to know if you'd like to toss double or quits?'

I laughed heartily. 'Very funny—anything for a laugh, these boys, eh?'

'No, no, he means it seriously. Do you want to?'

I would dearly have loved to, but I could only decline. If I had lost I had no means of paying off my creditors, who needed the money. I had to refuse; but my refusal cost me some esteem locally. Clearly I did not share the sporting spirit enjoyed by every true Greek.

The Greek works hard when he has to but his sense of urgency often does not match that of the foreigner. *Avrio,* the Greek manãna, is the first word one should learn, followed by *Thenverazi* (Not to worry) and *Etsiketsi* (It might go either way). When we needed some patio furniture we were determined to have it made in the local wrought iron which shows real craftsmanship, whereas poor quality unseasoned wood often mars carpentry. The faithful Taki once again assisted us, this time to the blacksmith's. This worthy pondered long over my wife's designs, showing an artist's interest and suggesting several variations and simplifications. The requirement and price were agreed and I asked Taki to enquire about the time needed for the work.

'About three days, he says.'

This was very satisfactory but I did not happen to go into town again for five days. I encountered Taki on the waterfront and asked him if he could accompany me again to take delivery.

'The blacksmith? Oh yes, I happened to be up there this morning. He hasn't started on your order yet.'

'Oh? Well, there isn't all that hurry, I suppose. But he did say three days, and that was five days ago if you remember, Taki.'

'Ah yes; but that's three days from when he decides to start the job, you see.'

I saw. The furniture was, I learned, actually made (and beautifully made) about six months later by which time we were in Singapore. *Thenverazi.*

The whole island operates on a similarly unreal basis, although tourism has unhappily altered some of the old standards. Even the animal life does not behave as we have come to expect. One season our villa was invaded by field mice. I purchased a massive traditional mouse-trap, baited it with a piece of brick-hard island cheese and left it on the kitchen floor. The next morning the cheese had been abstracted but the trap was unsprung. I fixed next night's cheese even more firmly on the spike, but by the next morning the process had been repeated. I checked the operation of the spring, reset it, replaced it on the floor and looked for a piece of cheese. There was none, so I retired to bed frustrated. The following morning the baitless trap had slain not one but two mice. I could only presume that finding no appetizing titbit, they had vented their indignation in the Greek manner by furious foot-stamping—with lethal results.

It will not have escaped the notice of my readers that I have become entirely enthralled by my island. It is not of course mine in the sense that I possess it, rather that it possesses me. Nor does it lie alone; there are many other islands within easy striking range, notably Skopelos, larger than Skiathos but more successful in its preservation of its pristine freedom from foreign invasion. It may seem odd for an Englishman to speak so, but then I am proud to say that I am also now officially a Skiathan. In 1972 I was honoured to be made an honorary citizen of Skiathos, only the second in its recorded history. I was not foolish enough to take this courteous gesture too seriously, but I naturally enquired of my local friends what particular privileges accompanied this honour? Droit de seigneur, jus primae noctis with the ladies of the island perhaps? Or at least free drinks in the local tavernas? No, no, they corrected me; the boot was quite on the other foot. It was up to the honorary citizen instead to acknowledge the tribute paid him by some token gift to the island; a shrine perhaps, or a church, or even a kliniko, a cottage hospital. The choice of course would be mine.

Fortunately my embarrassment was allayed by the fact that my friend Niko Konialides, a brother-in-law of Onassis whoh as a handsome holiday residence on the island, beat me to it by himself presenting a splendid small modern kliniko to the citizens. At the opening ceremony he enhanced his generosity by offering a gift of 10,000 drachmae (about £150) to the mother of the first Greek son to be delivered in the kliniko. A scene straight out of Compton Mackenzie naturally ensued, with the island's prospective fathers chasing their expectant wives up and down the steep streets of the town, jigging them up and down in impromptu dance, filling them up with ouzo and generally encouraging early production.

It is thus that I shall leave them for the time being, eccentric, unpredictable individualists, lovable fascinating companions, unconforming and uncaring for the conventions that confine so much of our own lives. In my imagination they live in eternal sunshine—we relish the thought that we shall constantly be revisiting them.

132

18 'Which, taken at the flood, leads on to . . .'

On my return to England in the spring of 1967, I embarked on the career pattern prescribed for me earlier, ie to be Director General of Organization (RAF) for about a year and then to be promoted to the Air Council as the Air Member for Supply and Organization. However, Chiefs of Air Staff change and with them sometimes come changes in such plans. It was with unalloyed delight that I learned from the new Chief, John Grandy, that in the summer of 1968 I was to become Commander in Chief of the RAF in Germany and Commander of NATO's Second Allied Tactical Air Force.

My successor as DGO was to be Air Vice Marshal Dicky Bird, and the Air Secretary invited us to find a mutually convenient date for hand-over in April. I had started in the post on 11 April 1967 and I thought it would be enjoyable to be able to boast that I had escaped from Whitehall in under a year; so I suggested 10 April to Dicky, who readily agreed. Only after consulting my diary did I realize that 10 April was in fact the Thursday before the Easter holiday break and Dicky would thus become entitled to four days London living-allowance for doing absolutely nothing. I called him and politely suggested that 15 April might be more suitable; but alas! he too had checked his diary, and 10 April stood. This was the only regret I felt on leaving Whitehall once again for foreign parts and once again a promotion.

Now that I had become Air Marshal and was later to be Air Chief Marshal, I suppose readers would imagine that one's heavy responsibilities, close involvement in matters of deep import and contact with the world's great men would add considerable interest, and perhaps length, to this narrative. In the event the contrary proves the case, because the very weight of those responsibilities and importance of the issues at stake mean that they are still often under the seal of confidentiality, many indeed still subjudice and unresolved and not suitable or even permissible for discussion or revelation in such pages as these. It would thus seem both consistent and inevitable to treat them as lightly and as light-heartedly as the rest of my story, although at the time it was often not easy to do so.

My Command in Germany was a dual one. Firstly, I was Commander in Chief of RAF Germany, a force of about 140 combat aircraft stationed in the northern part of that country. Secondly, I was Commander of NATO's Second Allied Tactical Air Force, a post usually but not invariably held by a British Officer. This comprised RAF Germany, the Belgian and Netherlands Air Forces, the half of the Luftwaffe based to the north of Germany, and the odd American Squadron.

The dual command arrangement presented only a few practical difficulties.

Under my national hat I had a British Air Vice Marshal Deputy C-in-C who bore much of that particular burden. Under my international hat my Chief of Staff was a Luftwaffe Major-General who did likewise. One adjusted one's own activity to whichever field produced the most pressing need at the time. There was one rather peculiar outcome. I occasionally had to write to myself wearing one hat, replace it smartly and reply under the other. For example in the (very rare) event of a disappointing performance by the British element in an operational exercise, I had, as Commander 2 ATAF, to address a courteous but firm rebuke to myself as C-in-C Germany. Then I had to reply in reverse order, with an apologetic but exculpatory letter, blaming ill luck, the weather or even undue interference from high command. It was rather like playing single-handed chess.

My Army opposite number, with whom I worked closely in every sense, had similar national and international positions. This generated no fewer than four Headquarters, which were all co-located in one edifice at Rhein-dahlen, west of Dusseldorf. This had been constructed with every kind of associated support facilities and domestic bits and pieces in an enormous cantonment, at a time when fortunately the Germans were still paying for this sort of thing. It is noteworthy that all such major building projects in contemporary Germany were if possible designed so that, should lasting peace ever come, they could revert to an alterative useful peacetime function. It is a matter of fact but naturally also a source of some jest, that in that happy event the Combined Headquarters was earmarked to serve as the biggest and best mental asylum in Germany.

A special extra-NATO responsibility for both British Cs-in-C lay in Berlin where the United Kingdom still acted as one of the four guarantor countries, the others being Russia, France and the USA. Each in theory had its own geographical Sector although passage between those of the three Western powers was quite free and unchallenged. Not so of course the Russian zone of East Berlin bounded by the notorious Wall and impassable except on very rare formal occasions by senior British officers. We did however maintain an inter-Service mission in Soviet territory, the RAF element of which came under my command; the Soviets had a similar mission in the British Army area of northern Germany. My wife could and regularly did obtain permission to penetrate the Wall and visit such places as Potsdam. On one such occasion she tripped on a kerbstone and fell, nastily scraping her leg. The East German bystanders could not have been more helpful and sympathetic, one particular little man not only slapping large sections of sticking plaster on the uncleansed wounds but also beamingly insisting on presenting her with a million Mark note as a token of personal esteem. Unfortunately it proved to have been printed in about 1924 and was therefore quite worthless, but this did not prevent them from exchanging happy greetings whenever their paths crossed again.

The RAF C-in-C had a pleasant house in Berlin overlooking the Havel lake and a majestic Mercedes car (to forestall cries of protest I hasten to add that all costs of our forces in Berlin are borne by the Federal German Budget). I found on my first arrival that this car was the subject of some controversy between my financial and equipment staffs. Being more than five years old it was officially due for replacement; but because it had been driven almost exclusively within West Berlin it had clocked up no more than 30,000 miles, more or less in its prime for a Mercedes. The argument was resolved when, upon my first formal visit to Mayor Schultz of West Berlin during which the full panoply of police escort, sirens and flying flags was deployed, my driver unfortunately skidded in an emergency stop on a wet road and took the car and ourselves straight up the back end of a police Land Rover. So I got a new Mercedes anyway.

Visits to Berlin were unhappily not too frequent and most of our time was spent at Rheindahlen, situated in a lowlying, foggy and somewhat featureless part of Germany. The work however was demanding and interesting and the company was excellent. I saw it as a primary duty to establish close and friendly relations with the Army and with my NATO staff. I say duty, but it was also a pleasure and neither presented any real difficulties. My Army colleague, Desmond Fitzpatrick, apart from his great personal charm, clearly saw that professionally we were closely interdependent and that any friction was bound to affect our operational efficiency. He left his subordinates in no doubt that he would not tolerate any such friction, as I did myself; and so consequently there was none.

Nor indeed did we have any real problems with our NATO colleagues, with whom both personal and professional relationships were of the best. Some of our allies whose countries and whose families had suffered all the anguish and hardship of occupation by the Germans naturally found it difficult to be fully at ease with them; but, rightly or wrongly, this applied less to ourselves, the Canadians and the Americans who had been spared that traumatic experience. My wife and I formed many close and lasting friendships with Germans, both in civilian and military life.

One of the warmest of these was with Johannes and Ursula Steinhoff. Steinhoff was the current Inspector General of the Luftwaffe, a man of great power and character but also with a well developed sense of humour. His personal history was remarkable. Towards the end of World War II, when in fact it was effectively lost, the Germans had introduced jet fighters into their air defence system (they would have done so earlier had not Hitler, fortunately for us, insisted on their initial use as tactical bombers). A wing of such aircraft, the Messerschmitt 262, was formed and manned exclusively by proven fighter aces, most of them of high rank. In the last weeks of the war Adolf Galland was leading this wing from an airfield in Bavaria to intercept the waves of daylight Allied bombers. As the wing took off, one aircraft crashed back on to the airfield and burst into a vast sheet of flame. The scanty fire services could no nothing; the pilot did not get out. Galland called the tower: ' Who was in that aircraft? '.

' I'm afraid it was General Steinhoff, Sir ' (they were close friends).

On landing back from the mission, Galland demanded to be taken to see Steinhoff's body.

' But, General, he is not dead. He is in the Station Sickquarters.'

The medical and hospital facilities for the Luftwaffe were of course by then in total chaos under overwhelming Allied bombing and the pressure of our advancing armies. Galland was driven to the improvised Sickquarters. After one look at Steinhoff who was most dreadfully burned and whose face had been flayed down to the skull itself, he turned to the young air force doctor in charge: ' Kill him '.

' Sir, I cannot do that.'

' Kill him, I say. No one can be permitted to live in such an appalling condition.'

But the doctor still refused, a remarkable performance in view of the rigid code of German discipline; and one for which Johannes Steinhoff is naturally very grateful to this day. After a prolonged period of suffering in the shambles of postwar Germany, when for 20 years he could not close his eyes in sleep for lack of eyelids, a series of 70 facial operations were performed on him, many of them by the RAF in the person of that great surgeon the late Air Vice Marshal Morley. His face is still terribly disfigured and scarred but the result is nevertheless almost miraculous. After the latest of these operations, the Steinhoffs happened to be staying with us at Air House. I asked him when the next was to be.

' No, Chris. I think I will not have any more. I think that must be the last.'

' By God, I know how you must feel. I just can't conceive how you have managed to withstand so many already.'

' No, no, it is not that. You see, it is just that I am afraid that if I have any more, I shall be made too good-looking, the girls will be all over me, and Ursie will become jealous.'

A remarkable couple. Her courage must have been just as great as his. During the period of his worst disfigurement, they produced a family of delightful children.

We had many other visitors at Air House, this being part of the accepted responsibilities of an overseas Commander in Chief. One is provided with a large and well staffed official house for the purpose and ours always seemed to be full. After about two years some Ministry inspectors called on my household to check, perfectly justifiably, whether my official entertainment allowance was being fully and properly spent. They enquired first how many guest meals had been served in the house during the period. The answer was about ten thousand. Since this amounted to about twelve a day on average, they expressed incredulity but my admirable chef, Sergeant Darler, had kept the books meticulously and the figure withstood scrutiny. To do them credit, the inspectors asked no further questions and took their departure briskly—presumably to forestall any bid for higher allowances.

Our guests were of all shapes and sizes, ages, nationalities, professions and of either sex. Some were less easy to handle than others. For example a visiting politician was discovered by my ADC packing away in his suitcase the drinks and cigarettes provided in his bedroom for overnight sustenance.

' Well, why not? ' he protested defensively. ' Your boss gets it all free, doesn't he? Taxpayer's paying after all, isn't he? '

Some people live in a world of their own cf the widespread belief that the

Services are provided with houses rent free. I even entertained one distinguished Headmaster who turned out to be convinced that Servicemen paid no income tax. I could only hope that he had not persuaded too many of his pupils to join the Armed Forces under such a false premise.

Unquestionably our most distinguished and delightful guest was Princess Anne whose visit to the Command in 1970 was by way of being her own major first solo. However such was her natural charm and enthusiasm that the whole programme of both official and unofficial functions went off without a hitch, indeed with a considerable swing. On departure she left us with a striking photograph of herself which took traditional pride of place on the grand piano. I had to rebuke my ADC for spending too much of his time gazing at it. It was, I pointed out, a waste of the taxpayer's money for a well paid officer to do so; furthermore, it was certainly bad for good order and discipline for us both to be doing so.

When we were not entertaining we were travelling. My own Command covered a pretty large area and there were many visits to be made to other Headquarters and to neighbouring forces. For this purpose I was initially provided with a Valetta aircraft, the pride and joy of my predecessors but now of such antiquity that when it was shortly retired it went straight into the RAF Museum at Hendon. It was replaced by an aircraft of equally ancient and honourable vintage, a de Havilland Heron. This was a smaller aircraft but boasted four tiny engines which hauled it through the sky at a cruising speed of about 150 knots. I initially christened it ' Snow White ' because it could just about accommodate seven dwarfs; but my crew naturally objected to flying about with such a name emblazoned on the fuselage. So I rechristened it *Quadriga*, which reference to the Concise Oxford Dictionary will show to mean ' an ancient chariot with four horses abreast '.

The appearance of this venerable vehicle on major occasions among the executive jets and other more modern conveyances enjoyed by our allies invariably aroused notice and comment (not always charitable, ' Did'ya make it yourself? '). One was irresistibly reminded of the passage in A. G. Macdonnell's *England, their England*, describing the arrival at the League of Nations Building in Geneva of the various national plenipotentiaries in their Cadillacs, Hispana-Suizas, Delages etc. The British representative drove up in the quiet dignity of a carriage and pair.

It was not only one's colleagues who found this aircraft somewhat of a surprise. Air traffic controllers were also occasionally at a loss. One evening we were climbing out of a Bavarian USAF base in filthy weather, with heavy icing, cloud and snow. We had already been despatched to 12,000 feet, although we had no oxygen, when the controller realized that the always congested German skies were even more crowded than usual and there were other aircraft on a converging course with our own.

' Sunspot 46, Sunspot 46 ' he called hurriedly. ' Immediate emergency climb to 14,000 feet to avoid traffic '.

This instruction we justifiably regarded as somewhat academic since we calculated that in our heavily iced-up condition such a manoeuvre would have taken 27 minutes, even assuming we could have accomplished it at all.

However, for the rest of my flying I was much more fortunate. The Command, previously largely equipped with the Hunter and the Canberra, was during my time converting to the much more exciting Harrier jump jet, Phantom F4 and Buccaneer. Their greatly superior performance much improved the operational effectiveness of the Command. Indeed the whole of NATO at this time made considerable similar advances. The Russian invasion of Czechoslovakia in August 1968 suddenly reawakened many a politician and financier to the harsh realities of the Soviet threat. For a brief while purse-strings were relaxed and hurried measures taken to restore the military balance which years of parsimony and apathy had so dangerously eroded.

My personal experience of that particular moment in history was somewhat unusual. I was roused from sleep at 3 am by a call from the Duty Officer telling me that the invasion was in full swing. I flung on my clothes and hurried down to the Operations Centre. My discretionary powers were limited by governmental policy but I took what precautionary measures were within them, and sat down to await guidance from above.

Nothing happened for 12 hours and more; absolutely nothing. I eventually decided to slip back to the house for a bath and a meal. No sooner had I arrived there than my Personal Staff Officer was on the line to tell me that an official envelope had arrived for me from the Ministry, marked ' Exclusive—To be opened only by Commander-in-Chief '.

' That'll be it, Barry ', I said. ' That'll be what we've been waiting for '.

' Well, Sir ', he hesitated, ' I'm not so sure. It doesn't seem to be sufficiently highly classified '.

' Oh, probably just a registry error ' I replied. ' Whip it up here immediately '.

The envelope was with me in five minutes. I ripped it open with trembling hands and impatiently scanned its contents. They read:

Sir,
I have the honour to inform you that owing to your failure to comply with paragraph 156, sub-paragraph 4(b) of regulations governing the conveyance of Senior Officers' Effects to Overseas Theatres, your claim for repayment expenses in this connection, amounting to £92.16.0 is disallowed in toto.
I have the honour to be, Sir, etc, etc

That was the sole communication I received from Whitehall throughout that particular crisis. At least it was nice to know I was not altogether forgotten by the great men there.

A somewhat bizarre incident occurred during the Command's re-equipment with the Phantom aircraft. One of our larger airfields was to close after the departure of its Canberra aircraft, for the completion of certain works-services necessary for the heavier, faster and more sophisticated Phantom. The manning of the station was naturally much reduced for that period, and on a bitterly cold snowy evening in early 1970 only a few airmen were still at work in one of the hangars.   Under a Flight Sergeant, they were dealing with the few remaining Canberras to make them serviceable for disposal. Four of these aircraft were standing outside on the snow-covered flight-line. A Corporal RAF policeman with his guard dog entered the Flight Sergeant's office to make a formal report of a minor security breach.   On checking the aircraft he had found one with its crew-access door open.   He had looked round inside with his torch, found nothing amiss and duly closed the door. The tail number of the aircraft was 491.   Having made his report, he went off on his rounds.   It is worth mentioning that he was newly arrived on the station and had no previous knowledge of the squadron.

The remaining airmen finished their work.   The conscientious Flight Sergeant decided that he had better check the offending aircraft himself before leaving.   He walked out to the darkened flight line with his torch, noting that there were no footprints in the snow other than those made by the Corporal and his dog.   All four aircraft were now securely closed up as the Corporal had reported; but the Flight Sergeant noticed with annoyance that none of them carried the tail number 491.

' Bloody fool ', he thought, ' Can't even take down a three figure number correctly '.

He returned to his office to enter in the Flight Log the result of his check. While doing so, he casually thumbed through the squadron record to see how the error over the number could have arisen.   Sure enough, there had been a 491.   It had crashed on just such a night exactly two years before, killing its crew.

That is the end of the story.   There is no follow up, no explanation—at least none that I like to accept.

Personally I am in no way psychic, but my wife is.   Shortly before leaving the Command, I was due to fly one of Bruggen's Phantoms on an air-to-ground firing sortie.   We were having lunch with some German friends. My wife asked if I really had to make this flight; she would rather I didn't. I did; and in the process took three large pigeons in my starboard engine at low altitude.

However the end of that story was a happy one.   Among my pleasanter souvenirs as I write is a six-inch high plastic dolly-bird.   She is clothed entirely in pigeon feathers which the technicians at Bruggen had later extracted from that same engine.

Such incidents were not uncommon, especially in Germany where at certain times of year the normal bird population is augmented by large migratory flocks.   When for example the geese were coming through, training operations had to be rerouted for mutual safe passage.   Additionally the confined airspace of West Germany and the Low Countries was over-crowded with large numbers of military aircraft as well as civil.   My wife on one occasion being flown in a helicopter on an official visit to a remote station, while proceeding at a few hundred feet above a Dutch canal was startled to note the flight of two 104 Starfighters beneath the helicopter, on a directly opposite course and at about 500 knots.   Her pilot remained impressively unperturbed but only, as it later turned out, because he had been quite unaware of their presence.

In spite of such hazards, as the year 1969 progressed the RAF in Germany was clearly approaching a remarkable flight safety record. Apart from some inevitable bird-strikes not one aircraft of well over a hundred flying in stringent operational conditions and all extremes of weather had been involved in an accident or even an incident (officialese for a minor accident); and this at a time when German Starfighters were sticking into the ground like darts all over the place and the RAF in the United Kingdom was regularly reporting the loss of Lightning and other aircraft. As the months went by and our record remained spotless an atmosphere of considerable tension naturally developed, and by December if anyone had even scratched the paint on an aircraft he would have been lynched. At last came 1 January 1970 and the record, unique for a tactical air force, was ours; we had not had a single unavoidable accident or incident in a full calendar year. I pressed all the buttons in sight to get the maximum public relations coverage.

We did not get a single line or mention in any newspaper, magazine or broadcasting medium. Once again one was forcibly reminded ' Good news is no news '.

I felt I had to try my prentice hand at the 104 Starfighter, then enjoying an unhappy record in the Luftwaffe for its almost daily crashes, enthusiastically publicized in the Press. A point that was never brought out however was that the Germans had more than eight hundred of this type of aircraft, while some of the smaller NATO airforces had only two or three dozen. Thus even if the Germans lost twenty for every one by those airforces, the percentage was about the same. My then Chief of Staff, Major-General Herbert Wehnelt, at the age of fifty-three flew the 104 regularly, competently and confidently while doing his staff job. However I somewhat cravenly declined his kindly offer to teach me to fly one (even though our combined ages by coincidence would have been 104). I was put through my paces by a young Dutch instructor and found it not very different from most modern aircraft.

Our time in Germany approached its end all too rapidly. Because the holding of high command is of such importance in a senior officer's career and because such appointments are now so few, the RAF quite rightly limits one's length of tour; and anything over two years may be regarded as a bonus. I could count myself lucky to have had such a bonus (of four months), but nevertheless we were very sad when the time came to say goodbye—even though some of the farewell ceremonies and occasions were both enjoyable and memorable, including at one extreme a full scale traditional torchlight parade, a *Grosser Zuperfenstriech*, by the German Armed Forces, an honour which Desmond Fitzpatrick and I were the first foreign officers to receive; at the other extreme driving away somewhat alcoholically from a British base at the controls of a branch-line railway engine, with my wife as an equally impaired co-pilot.

My next appointment, which carried with it promotion to Air Chief Marshal, was a recently created tri-Service one, Chief of Personnel and

Logistics. Translated from Whitehall jargon, this meant that one had overall responsibility for all the people, the supplies and the movements of the British armed forces. It was clearly not going to be a light load.

The post of Chief of Defence Staff had been in existence since the mid-1950s. In recent years the need had become apparent to relieve him of some of his burden to allow him to concentrate on the major issues of policy and operations. For a while he was given a functionary called the Deputy Chief of Defence Staff (P & L); this later became the Chief Adviser in Personnel and Logistics; and in 1970 Mr Healey decided to raise the responsibility and authority of the office by making it executive rather than advisory and giving its holder a seat on our premier military committee, the Defence Council.

The Chiefs of Staff, reacting as always to any hint of centralized authority with all the nervousness shown in a nunnery at the arrival of the milkman, produced a rather peculiar compromise by which CPL attended all their committee meetings but not as a member. Since however they were not in the habit of putting issues to a vote and since CPL was as free to speak as anyone else present, the practical effect of this, or indeed the thinking behind it, was not easy to determine.

Nevertheless although CPL's responsibilities were great they remained only to supervise and co-ordinate, since each single Service conducted its own day-to-day business in personnel and supply; and the office was one of singular frustration, even by Whitehall standards, since it directly controlled no Defence money, which continued to be allotted to Single Service votes. One could thus in effect determine what ought to be done but other people had to do it; and only too often, in the nicest possible way and with the best possible motives, they found themselves unable to oblige.

Nevertheless the job was one of unparalleled interest and remarkable variety (as Chairman of the Defence Medical Services Committee I even found myself more or less Top Doctor, though I received no specialist emoluments in the appointment). The inter-Service environment contributed much to both the interest and variety. Inter alia I was blessed with the almost unique privilege of having a Flag Lieutenant; and there is nothing better for the ego than being able to call ' Flags! ' from behind one's office desk in a tone combining dignity, tradition and kindly authority. One worked closely with, and admired the skills and techniques of senior civil servants and of politicians. In particular I was lucky enough to be in regular touch with our then Secretary of State, Peter Carrington, whose energy and comprehension were only matched by his wit and good-humour.

On one occasion we were all engaged on a large annual NATO simulated crisis-game, in which for the greater part of its course junior officers and officials play the parts of the great men of defence and government. During the final period, the great men themselves join in. They were being duly informed on how the imaginary exercise had gone so far, when the senior briefer in the Chiefs of Staff Conference Room completed this up-dating, and recommenced:

' . . . and now, gentlemen, we may say that the exercise goes live '.

141

At this precise moment a large IRA bomb exploded just off Whitehall. The building shook, the windows rattled, the sirens and bells of ambulances and fire engines reached a crescendo.

After a pretty pregnant pause, I ventured to address the Secretary of State: ' Do you not think, my Lord, that this business of "going live" can be carried a little too far? '.

He fixed me with his owl-like and impassive gaze.

' If you are windy, CPL, you may hide under the table. Let us continue with the briefing.'

In spite of such interruptions we kept at our labours, and in my own fields of responsibility we made much progress. The ' military salary ' was already a fait accompli. We gained agreement that it should be more regularly and consistently reviewed as inflation hit it. Officers' pensions were much improved. The period of review was reduced from two years to one; the qualifying age for such review was reduced from 60 to 55; and increments directly linked with rises in the cost of living were built in. The pensions of NCOs and other ranks, which had until then merited that much over-used adjective ' derisory ', were greatly increased, in some cases almost doubled.

On the logistic side, we moved everything and everyone (except the hamsters) out of and back into Malta with the precision and timing of a corps de ballet. We at last began to make real advances in standardizing equipment not only between our own Services but within NATO as a whole. Our codification system won the admiration of industry; and our computers led the field.

It was all hard slogging work, but no work is intolerable if the results can be seen and can be seen to justify it. Ours did, and, particularly on the pay and pension side, it was gratifying how many people acknowledged it.

19 '... the Ejection Seat'

Thus at the beginning of 1973 I was able to look back with reasonable self-satisfaction on two years of considerable professional achievement. I say ' self ', but of course that achievement was largely attributable to the expert and dedicated work by the members of my own and associated staffs, both uniformed and civil. It all looked pretty good although obviously more problems lay ahead, which we looked forward to tackling.

In this atmosphere of comparative euphoria it came as a considerable surprise and disappointment to be informed by the RAF authorities that I was to be prematurely retired at the beginning of 1974 at the early age, for an Air Chief Marshal, of 56. It was explained to me that the pressure for promotion of younger aspirants was such that it had become necessary to confine an individual to one appointment in that rank—an explanation to which I naturally lent a sympathetic ear until I found later that it did not seem to apply to my friends and contemporaries. Perhaps understandably, I gave some expression to that surprise and disappointment.

' Ah well! not to worry ', was the bland reply. ' It'll give you time to write a book '.

So I did. And this is it.